Voyages
with my
Grandfather

William D. Hanna

Copyright © 2020 William D. Hanna

The moral right of the author has been asserted.

Apart from any fair dealing for the purposes of research or private study, or criticism or review, as permitted under the Copyright, Designs and Patents Act 1988, this publication may only be reproduced, stored or transmitted, in any form or by any means, with the prior permission in writing of the publishers, or in the case of reprographic reproduction in accordance with the terms of licences issued by the Copyright Licensing Agency. Enquiries concerning reproduction outside those terms should be sent to the publishers.

Matador
9 Priory Business Park,
Wistow Road, Kibworth Beauchamp,
Leicestershire. LE8 0RX
Tel: 0116 279 2299
Email: books@troubador.co.uk
Web: www.troubador.co.uk/matador
Twitter: @matadorbooks

ISBN 978 1838593 926

British Library Cataloguing in Publication Data.
A catalogue record for this book is available from the British Library.

Printed and bound in the UK by TJ International, Padstow, Cornwall
Typeset in 12pt Minion Pro by Troubador Publishing Ltd, Leicester, UK

Matador is an imprint of Troubador Publishing Ltd

For my grandchildren:

"I want you… to remember me
And what the wind-tousled wren has been saying
All day long from fence posts and the fuchsia depths,
A brain-rattling bramble-song inside a knothole."

From "The Wren" by Michael Longley

Contents

Preface — vii
Family Chart — xii

Part One   1880–1909 — 1
We Presbyterians — 3
The Boy Who Was Given Away — 9
Annie Higginson – AHB — 21

Part Two   1909–1953 — 31
The Ambivalent Imperialist — 33
The Lonely Road — 35
Village Folk of India — 45
Mahatma Gandhi – The Great Soul — 49
The Prevailing Word — 56
Robert Boyd's Rhetoric Reviewed — 59

Part Three   1936-1937   65
Letters from Around the World   67
Eyebright   70
Canada to Japan   76
Korea and Manchuria   86
China, Singapore and Malaya   102
Return to India   112
A Monster Pounces   126
Anand, Surat and Broach   133
"Fooled" Again   139
Homeward Bound   147

Part Four   2010–2019   155
Bangladesh/Phule Phule   157
Burma: The Path of Valour   159
Gujarat   167
Drumbo   180
Postscript   184
Bibliography   187

Preface

This story is about my grandfather, Robert H Boyd (1880–1957), and how I got to know him fifty years after his death.

I was two and a half years old when Grandpa Boyd went away. He no longer sat in his green armchair smiling down at me. He reappeared later, in two pictures above the drawing-room mantelpiece. One was a sepia photograph, set in a tortoiseshell oval frame, showing a young man in a black frock-coat, with a beautiful lady in white by his side. They were standing together in a garden. These, I was told, were my grandparents, who had been missionaries in India. The photo was taken on their wedding day in Surat in 1915. The other photo showed Grandpa, who from now on I will call RHB, his face older and his hair white, looking confidently at the camera. He was dressed in eighteenth century clothes, black satin robes with tassels, white lace around his neck, and black shoes with silver buckles on his feet. That was RHB as Moderator of the General Assembly of the Presbyterian Church of Ireland in 1947.

As I grew up, in Belfast, Gran read to me from RHB's books, and I learnt that he was a well-known writer. Over the years my mother gave me precious objects that had belonged to him – his British Empire stamp collection, and a silver locket in which he kept a curl of her golden hair that he cut on her eighteenth birthday. RHB – grandfather, missionary and moderator – has stayed with me all my life.

My mother often told me that when I was a baby lying in my pram I was so placid that RHB would ask, 'Can he kick?' That is the only question that I know RHB asked about me. But I've always had questions about him. In 2007, fifty years after RHB died, I decided to find out more. I asked my mother and her brothers, Uncles Robin and Billy, to tell me what they remembered, and I visited relatives in County Armagh where RHB came from. I read some of his books and found more in libraries. There was even an article about RHB on the internet, and I was thrilled to find a new study of his writing entitled *Ambivalent Imperialism: The Missionary Rhetoric of Robert Boyd*.

My search became a journey, a voyage with my grandfather, with his books as guide. In 2010 my diplomatic career took me to Bangladesh, where I was accredited as Ambassador of the European Union. In RHB's time, Bangladesh, then East Bengal, was part of India. During my posting to the Indian sub-continent I was able to visit Gujarat, where RHB worked and where his eldest son, Jack, and my mother, Honor, were born. I was also the first in the family to visit Myanmar/Burma, where Uncle Jack was killed during the Second World War.

2010 was also the year my mother died and I became a grandfather. It seemed important to record my journey with RHB and pass on the story to my own grandchildren. RHB is part of our DNA. For example, I have inherited his white hair, his passion for travel and his impatience. My grandchildren come from the same roots, and each one takes a little after him. In some of them I see a Boyd resemblance. So, this story of their great-great grandfather is for them. May it skip, like a skimming stone, across our five generations and a hundred and forty years.

Missionaries are not popular figures today and many people think they were misguided. Contemporary readers may not share or understand RHB's religious beliefs, and may be put off by the brash dogmatism of his early writing. But after many years of studying him, I remain fascinated by his steadfast character. RHB is an entertaining travelling companion, and it is a joy to pass on his story to future generations.

RHB lived in a different world, at a time of great upheaval. He wrote his first book in Edwardian times at the height of the British Empire. On my odyssey with him, I have seen how he always stuck to his beliefs, but nevertheless changed his attitude to other people. He found it a rich experience to live in a poor country. He came to love India as much as his native Ireland. He met the greatest Indian, Mahatma Gandhi, several times and both admired and criticised him. He also got to know and sympathise with the poorest Indians, their lives and problems. He made sure that many village folk in India were given new opportunities, through education, health and agriculture.

We, who are his descendants, are far richer in worldly goods than RHB ever was, or desired to be. He knew, to use the biblical analogy, that "it is easier for a camel to go through the eye of a needle than for a rich man to enter the Kingdom of God". He followed the commandments of the New Testament. The first commandment is to love God "with all your heart and soul and mind", and the second commandment is "to love your neighbour as yourself". Many people today, including world leaders, claim to be Christians, but have forgotten this simple but demanding teaching.

In this story I draw on conversations with RHB's children – my mother and uncles. I quote his books and an unpublished memoir, entitled *While I Remember*. I also quote two diaries written by my grandmother, and I try to get to know her better too. When the life and times of RHB remind me of episodes from my childhood or my career I tell some of my own stories. In a way this book about my grandfather is also the first instalment of my own memoirs. In Part Three, I reproduce the letters RHB wrote, in a beautiful, legible hand, to his children, as he went round the world in 1936–1937. The letters give a better idea about RHB and his world than any other source. When he writes to his children he springs to life, and I want to ask him lots of questions. Where did you first meet Gran? What was it like to share a platform and sing hymns with Mahatma Gandhi? What did you think of the Amritsar massacre? I'd also have loved to tell RHB some of my own stories, such as how I once sang with the prime minister of Bangladesh.

My thanks go to Justin Livingstone, who allowed me to include an extract from his study of RHB's writing, and Michael Longley, my English teacher at "Inst" who allowed me to quote from his poem, "The Wren". I am also indebted to Alexander McCall Smith, who offered me wise advice and gifted me a copy of one of RHB's finest books, *Village Folk of India*. Geoff Randal encouraged me to complete this story and helped with the proof-reading. My uncle, Dr William Boyd, along with his brother, the late Dr Robin Boyd, shared many memories of their father with their nephew. Like their father they made fascinating and meticulous observations. I apologise for the errors, which are all mine, as is the selection of material. My wife, Paola Fornari, understood more than anyone else what this journey with my grandfather meant. She listened to me talk about RHB, over many years, journeyed with me to India, and Myanmar/Burma, and greatly assisted with the editing.

WH
Brussels, 2020

Family Chart

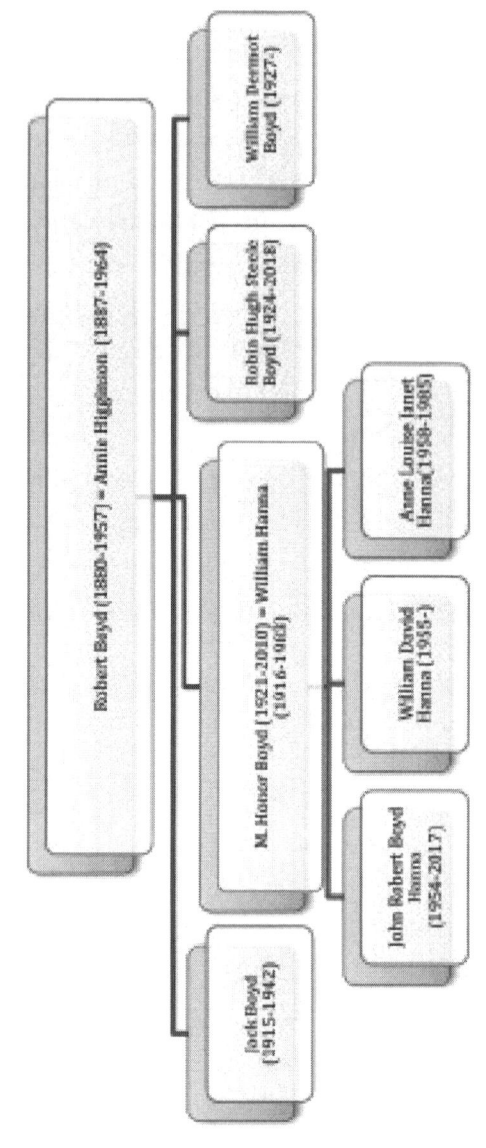

PART ONE

1880–1909

We Presbyterians

Here is the entry about RHB I found on the Internet:

Boyd, Robert (1880–1957), Presbyterian minister, was born 10 September 1880 in Tullyvallen, near Newtownhamilton, Co. Armagh, but was brought up by his uncle in Drumgaw, Co. Armagh. His father George Boyd was a farmer and his mother was Annie Boyd (née Gray). He attended school in Armagh and entered Queen's College Belfast, graduating BA from the Royal University of Ireland in 1902. He studied theology in Princeton, New Jersey, for two sessions, then completed his course in Assembly's College, Belfast. Licensed by Armagh presbytery (1906), he became secretary to the board of missions, and in 1909 was ordained as a missionary to India. He ministered especially to young people in Gujarat without a furlough for ten years because of the outbreak of the First World War. In 1919 his administrative work received official recognition from the Indian government. In 1920 he became principal of Stevenson Theological College, Ahmedabad, but was recalled in 1921 to Belfast to become Convenor of the Foreign Missions Board of the General Assembly. He remained in this post till 1954, becoming widely known for his lectures and preaching, and in 1936 received the degree of DD honoris causa from the Presbyterian Theological Faculty of Ireland. On 2 June 1947 he was installed as moderator of the general assembly. He undertook the responsibilities of the moderatorship again for a short time in 1949, when his successor died before completing his term. Boyd published several books, including A Garland of Memories *and* Path of Valour. *These dealt mainly with mission work; the first contains some autobiographical information. He married (7 January 1915) Annie Higginson of Dunmurry, near Belfast. One of their three sons was killed in Burma in the Second World War; the others both became Presbyterian ministers, and the only daughter married a minister. Robert Boyd died 14 October 1957 in Belfast.*

There, today and for future generations, is a summary of RHB's life. When I read it I wanted to know more. Who really was RHB? What was he like? Why was he brought up by his uncle? How did he become a missionary? What was the work recognised by the Indian government? I knew

RHB had met Gandhi, but where and how, and what did they talk about?

I already knew something of RHB's background. He was an Ulster Scot, who would sometimes refer to himself as Scots/Irish, as well as British. His forebears migrated three hundred years ago from south-west Scotland, across the narrow channel to the north of Ireland. The clan Boyd is well known in Scotland. A Robert Boyd was at Robert the Bruce's side at the Battle of Bannockburn in 1314. The king rewarded him with lands and titles in Ayrshire. However economic hardship and religious persecution in the seventeenth and eighteenth centuries led many Scots, including Boyds, to seek their fortune abroad, in Ireland or America.

RHB was brought up as a member of the Presbyterian Church in Ireland, the largest of the Protestant denominations, closely linked, until recently, to the Church of Scotland. Presbyterians trace their roots back to the sixteenth century Protestant reformers Jean Calvin of Geneva and John Knox of Scotland. They rejected practices of Catholicism that were not based on the Bible. They wanted a direct relationship with God, rather than having clergymen intercede on their behalf. To us today these forefathers may seem like dour and miserable men, preachers of a gloomy religion. The early reformers believed that people did not have free will to make choices in life. Each person's destiny was already decided, and only an elected few would be saved in the next life. As a child RHB was exposed to this fundamentalist Presbyterianism by his uncle, although his aunt attended a more tolerant mainstream church.

Presbyterianism also has attractive features, including democratic government and no hierarchy. Each Church chooses its own minister. The congregation elects elders who attend a presbytery (hence the name Presbyterians). A general assembly is presided for one year only by an elected moderator.

One day in the 1880s, when RHB was a boy, he witnessed this local democracy in action when his church had to choose a new Minister. He described the selection process in his memoir *While I Remember*.

> *The vacancy was hard to fill, and during it there were some lively scenes. I vividly recall one in which Mr T.W. Hewton, an elder, played what was to me the leading part. There had been a long discussion in which, to the embarrassment of the gentle moderator, the Rev Silas Wilson, but the great enjoyment of lads like me, a number of people had taken part. Mr Hewton, who sat near the back of the church, stepped forward. He was lame and dragged one foot a little. His voice was clear and resonant and it rang like a bell. 'Moderator, I demand a poll.' Having said that he returned to his seat. I was terrified by the thought of what Mr Newton might do with a pole. My aunt, who knew something about ecclesiastical terms, set my fears at rest. In the end we got a minister, the Rev David Millar, who was worth waiting for.*

A century earlier in Ireland such freedom of religion had been denied. The established church was Anglican, and

Presbyterians were persecuted for their beliefs. Many so-called "dissenters" emigrated to the United States, where they were free to worship as they wished. They were among the leaders of the American Revolution of the 1770s and some of them signed the US Declaration of Independence. Others who remained, particularly in Belfast and County Antrim, were influenced by the ideas of the French Revolution of 1789 – Liberty, Equality and Fraternity. They became leaders of the Society of United Irishmen that brought together Presbyterians and Catholics in the 1798 rebellion against Britain. The rebellion failed, and some of the rebels were hanged.

RHB grew up in this Presbyterian tradition in County Armagh at the end of the nineteenth century, as I did later in Belfast in the 1960s.

Ours was a deeply religious family, at a time and in a country where religion mattered. Presbyterian ministers were all around me. RHB was the most important, because he had been a moderator. There was also my father, William Hanna, and my maternal uncles, Robin Boyd and Billy Boyd. And there were many other ministers and missionaries on both sides of the family.

In Northern Ireland of the 1960s, Presbyterians had long ceased to be discriminated against. That was still the lot of our Catholic neighbours and the main cause of Northern Ireland's "Troubles".

Our house was called a manse and I am a Son of the Manse. A manse is the residence of a Presbyterian minister, provided by his church during his working life. Windsor Manse is a massive red-bricked house that still stands beside Windsor Presbyterian Church on the main

Lisburn Road in Belfast. The Manse was bitterly cold in winter, with the limited central heating usually turned off because it was too expensive to run. We either shivered or wore Aran knitted jumpers.

Our lives at home revolved around religion. We went to Sunday School, and then to church. We studied the Bible, said grace at mealtimes, and prayed together as a family. My father wore his clerical collar on weekdays. On Sunday after breakfast he tucked two starched white bands under the collar and put on cassock, black silk robes and a degree hood. By the time he left the Manse in this fancy dress he had become in my eyes a transformed and holy person.

On Sundays we weren't supposed to play cards, play outside or watch TV, with the exception of *Songs of Praise*. However, we could enjoy ourselves exploring the Manse. In the attic there was a trunk that overflowed with RHB's Presbyterian ceremonial clothes, and we were allowed to dress up in them. As well as the robes, there was a frock-coat, gaiters, a pair of tails, and a flowing Inverness cape. My brother, John Hanna – whose middle names were Robert Boyd after our grandfather – wore the cape to school at the beginning of the 1970s. He looked magnificent and eccentric.

The Boy Who
Was Given Away

In 2008 I returned to Europe after eight years posted abroad. My mother had become frail and was beginning to lose her memory. It seemed the right time to find out more about RHB, while those who knew him best were still around to tell the story.

I asked Uncle Billy, who told me this:

'RHB came from a family of nine. He was given away as a child and never felt anything warm towards his father or mother. He was first given to an old man who drank. Then later he was handed over to a nicer lady, an aunt who took the boy away.'

Uncle Billy also put me in contact with Boyd relatives still living in Loughgall, County Armagh. In August that year we spent a family holiday nearby, in Rostrevor, County Down, and one day I drove over to Loughgall. This is beautiful rolling countryside, with small round hills – called drumlins – criss-crossed by high hedges. On my way there I was struck by how similar were the names of my father's home village, Loughgiel in County Antrim, and my grandfather's, Loughgall, County Armagh.

I paid a call on a cousin, Hannah Hutchinson, née Boyd. We looked at each other and straightaway each of us saw a family resemblance. We both had a full head of grey hair and a high forehead. She reminded me of Kay Taylor, RHB's niece, whom we met in California when we visited the United States in 1996. It is heart-warming when you see a family trait in the faces of relatives – whether it's a new baby or an old lady.

I told Hannah Hutchinson that my hair started to turn grey when I was thirty. She wasn't surprised.

'Sure your grandfather went grey at a young age, and, as for his mother, well, she was born grey.'

I stared at her. Then she added, 'Her maiden name was Grey.'

She laughed. I guess I had fallen for a long-standing family joke.

Hannah explained that she was the daughter of Samuel Boyd, a cousin of RHB's, but who was "like a brother to him". She said that George and Annie Boyd's family farm was too poor to support all nine children. RHB was given away to different relatives, first at the age of five, and again when he was nine. The second time he went to live with Sam Boyd. Hannah told me that three of Sam Boyd's children died, in quick succession, of diphtheria, for which there was at that time no cure, leaving just two, her father, "the young Sam", and Aunt Maria.

So there was room to spare in Uncle Sam's household and RHB was sent, to replace the cousins who had been lost, and to grow up at their farm at Drumgaw, four miles from Armagh. He and his cousin Sam would sometimes ride on a bicycle back to his old home at Tullyvarren, the biggest townland in Ireland, which today stretches across the border.

When I returned from Armagh, I asked my mother more about this story. She told me that RHB would recall as a child overhearing adults talking about his future – including the words "what about the boy?" from the first uncle, "who drank".

'Then a lady came and took him away, and that would have been Sam Boyd's mother.'

The story of RHB's early days became clearer later when Uncle Billy showed me a copy of *While I Remember*. It starts at Tullyvarren, where RHB describes what it was like to live with a succession of uncles and aunts.

> *I don't remember leaving home at Tullyvallen, Newtownhamilton, to live with my aunt at Middletown. She was my father's twin sister, and her husband was Mr John Carlisle. He was a native of County Monaghan and was a member of the reformed Presbyterian Church.*
>
> *John Carlisle was an interesting man. I do not know how much education he received in his youth, and I cannot remember him reading many books except the Bible, Fore's Book of Martyrs and*

the Pilgrim's Progress. He was strict about family worship, at which he not only read the scriptures and prayed but also sang from the book of Psalms. He read two lines of a psalm at a time and then sang them. Whether they were sung to suitable tunes or not I do not know, for I am quite sure that I was tuneless till I was at least nine years of age. He was a great controversialist and many an argument I heard with visitors or neighbours on the doctrine of election and on various aspects of Roman Catholicism. An evangelist came once to Middletown to hold meetings. I went to one of them but all I remember about it is that the evangelist afterwards came to our house to discuss and debate free will and predestination with my uncle.

When he went to the Presbyterian Church he always sat through the singing of the paraphrases and he taught me to do the same. One day I was alone at church. The Rev William Ingram, a fine-looking man with a powerful voice, conducted the service. When I was questioned at home about the service I reported on the text and on the fact that he had not "given out a paraphrase". That was a good mark for Mr Ingram. He had however a tendency to something worse than paraphrases which almost ruined his ministry, but that failing would have been judged leniently by John Carlisle. I was told that as he drove the minister past a halfway house one Sunday he pointed to it with his whip and said that he remembered the time when they used to stop there for a glass of spirits. He added, 'I never paid for it on the Lord's day.'

A few memories of Middletown remain with me. There was an interval of half an hour between the closing of Sunday school and the beginning of the morning service. As a rule it was a lively time for us somewhere in the churchyard or near it. One day we remained in the church during the interval, and under provocation, or in response to a challenge or incitement, I went into the pulpit and pretended to be the minister. Someone gave the alarm "he's coming", he being the teacher or the minister. I closed the Bible and descended in haste, bringing one of the pulpit lamps with me. It crashed on the tiles below like the crack of doom. All the boys gathered round the fragments, held an inquest on them and conducted a trial, at the close of which I was assured that in due course I would be hanged.

I lived an isolated kind of life at home with a couple who were past middle life. When I was about nine years old my aunt met with an accident which laid her aside for a short time. The symptoms that remained gave rise to suspicion and I have a vivid recollection of the day on which the local doctor gave a positive opinion. An operation was performed, but it was not successful, and after some weeks of suffering she passed away and was laid to rest in the church at Middletown. The coming of uncles and aunts whom I had seldom seen before occupied my attention so fully that I did not take in the meaning of what had happened. When I was told that I was to leave Middletown I was thrilled by the prospect of what lay before me rather than saddened by what

I was to leave behind, and I bade my uncle John Carlisle goodbye in what must have seemed to him a very casual way.

It was arranged that I should go to live with an uncle and aunt at Drumgaw near Armagh. The reason for that decision was that they had recently lost three of their own children: a boy and two girls from diphtheria. It was a blow from which they did not recover for a long time, from which indeed my aunt never fully recovered her health. At Drumgaw I became one of the family. My Uncle Samuel and Aunt Hannah were more to me than parents, and my two cousins were closer than brothers and sisters.

Life in the country was full of interest, and as I grew up and became responsible for certain bits of work and lent a hand when an extra push had to be made, I enjoyed myself fully. A steady hand was at the helm in Drumgaw. There was a time for everything, and everything was done at the right time and in the right way. We got up when the factory horn blew at Milford, two or three miles away. It was dark and cold in the winter, but all the chores were done before it was time for the horses and men to go to the fields. Work never fell in arrears. The discipline was reasonable. The yoke was easy, for my uncle was a light-hearted man. He was industrious and efficient, but his work did not crush him beneath its burden. He suffered acutely from attacks of lumbago, but they were only like passing clouds. Naturally he had a merry heart, and I spent more time in horseplay with him than with any other person. My aunt was *of a more nervous cast. She may have been different before the loss of her children, but from the time I knew her she was tortured by nervousness. She was a large-hearted woman who delighted in giving, and apart for the affliction that harassed her she was as placid as a lake on a summer evening.*

In spite of all the religious observance, RHB was growing up in rural Ireland at a time when ancient superstitions were widely believed:

I once heard or thought I heard what was called "a warning". Something fell upstairs in a room over the kitchen. I was sent up to find out what it was and to put it right. I found everything in its place, especially the object that was thought to have fallen. When I reported the result of my search there was only one opinion about the occurrence: it was "a warning". Next morning news came by post that an aunt in Newtownhamilton was seriously ill, and arrangements were made to visit her without delay. A year later I heard another warning like the stroke of a cane on a table. Before daylight a messenger was at the door to announce the death of a near relative. Again seniors gravely, and as a matter of course, declared that the stroke I heard was "a warning". When the ill news came the only comment was, "Didn't I tell you?"

Newtownhamilton was on the edge of County Armagh, right where the border between Northern Ireland and the Republic would later be drawn. People of two different traditions, Protestants and Catholics, lived side by side. The Protestants' hero was King William of Orange, who defeated King James at the Battle of the Boyne in 1690. RHB was once taught an important lesson about living with his Catholic neighbours.

> *The number of Protestant children in the village was very small, but there was a Protestant school to which a fair number of boys and girls came from the country. I lived an isolated kind of life at home, with an elderly couple who were past middle life, and anything I ever heard about political parties or politics was on a rather remote plane. The worst language I ever heard applied to a Roman Catholic at home was, when in controversy with one, my uncle used the words "your sort" that suggested a deep cleavage. At school, however, I learnt from boys that were not reared in the covenanting atmosphere that there were other ways of referring to the majority of their neighbours and all that they stood for. And one day, not knowing what I meant, but merely repeating a slogan that I had picked up, I replied to one of my Roman Catholic playmates who had used popular words about King William, by substituting "the Pope" for the King. The fat was in the fire for he turned informer. My "bad words" came to the ears of Miss McNamee, one of the kindest of women from whose dairy we got our milk. When I went for the evening supply she sent me home empty-handed. It did not mollify her to say that my evil words were only a sort of tit for tat, a repetition of what I had heard from one of her sort. Home I had*

> *to go and explain why the milk jug was empty. I was taught a lesson of how to live in Rome and the door of the dairy was opened to me again.*

Sadly, not everyone in Northern Ireland was taught or learnt Miss McNamee's lesson. Antagonism between Protestants and Catholics has continued to be passed down from generation to generation. One day, in the early 1960s, when I was seven or eight, as I walked alone near my home in Belfast, I was stopped by two big boys who asked me if I was a Protestant or a Catholic. I didn't know which I was, nor the wisest answer to give, so I ran to escape their grasp. A few years later hatred spilled over into violence, and from 1969–1995 more than three thousand people were killed, often just because they were of the opposite religion, caught in the wrong place at the wrong time. After all this madness the murderers finally relented and the British and Irish governments, with support from the United States and the European Union, ensured that a Peace Agreement was signed. I had come to believe that I would never see peace in Northern Ireland in my lifetime. Today I pray that people will protect this agreement and do nothing that would bring us back to the dark days of violence.

But back to RHB. What effect did growing up away from his family have on him? My mother told me that in his later years RHB did not feel any warmth towards his own mother, and did not even greet her with a kiss.

It must have been hard for RHB's parents to raise a family of nine and for the children to be separated. Four of them migrated to the United States, as Uncle Billy explained in an e-mail to me.

RHB's brothers and sisters: -

Mark	emigrated in the nineties to Macbain, then little more than a crossroads, in Michigan and stayed there all his life. Married, three children, George, Kathryn, William all of whom brought up children.
Joseph	also to America, married, widowed, no children.
Samuel	worked for tea importers in Glasgow, back injured, came back to live in Newtownhamilton, Co. Armagh. Married, no children.
Robert	you know.
William	farmer on the home farm, later moved to Loughgall, married with one daughter. Georgie married Herbert Freeburn. They still live on the farm – three of a family married and scattered.
Georgina [Ena]	nurse. Married Andrew (who served in WW1, rubber planter in Malaya, served in WW2, prisoner on Burma Railway, retired to Donaghadee). No children. Andrew survived his wife some years.
Florence	married Ed Gray. They emigrated to Canada and farmed the Prairie near Edmonton. No children.
Margaret	office worker in Belfast, married Tom Reid, insurance broker, lived Ravenhill Road. Retired to bungalow near Bangor. Aunt Margaret died too soon. No issue.
Hannah	looked after elderly relative too long in Co Armagh. At last married Francis Whitfield and emigrated to New York, NY and lived happily in a tiny apartment. They were devoted to a company of very dedicated "disciples".

As he recounts in his letters RHB met up with his brother Mark and sisters Florence and Ena when he travelled around the world in 1936–7.

RHB's memoirs include stories of his schooldays. Gibson's private school in Armagh seems straight out of Dickens. Mr Gibson is a well-intentioned gentleman who tries to keep order by sitting in the middle of the classroom. He wears a wide-brimmed hat, into which the children throw paper pellets, when he is looking the other way. In upstairs rooms, Gibson has a pair of young assistants who are incompetent and sadistic. Young RHB protests when the assistant teachers punish him unfairly and give him hundreds of lines to write. He protests again when they discover his efforts to write three lines at once. They finally give him Euclid to write out.

Mr Gibson spots the potential in young RHB and tells him that he could become a moderator one day, if only he stops dreaming and applies himself to his studies. Two generations later, my primary school teachers gave me a similar message. Miss Strahan and Mr Lockett told me I should "hitch my wagon to a star".

As for pretending to be a minister in the pulpit, this game was also passed down to RHB's children and grandchildren. Uncle Billy reminded me of this in a recent letter. He recalled that in his generation, 'Robin preached, Honor was the congregation, Jack excused himself. I took up the collection.'

In my generation I was the one to lead the service, in the Manse drawing room on Sunday afternoons. I made a pretend pulpit from a nest of teak tables and drafted in my brother and sister as both acolytes and congregation.

I wanted to be a minister when I grew up, like my father and grandfather before me. That was not to be, but the oratorical skills I practised from a young age later came in handy in my chosen profession.

After my trip to Armagh, I visited Uncle Robin in Edinburgh and quizzed him more about his father's early life. He told me that when RHB went to Queen's University, Belfast in 1899 he met and was inspired by a missionary called Paton and he signed a declaration committing himself to become a missionary. Many years later Uncle Robin married Paton's granddaughter, Aunt Frances.

It was also at Queen's University that RHB first came into contact with the Higginsons. Willie Higginson was the son of John Higginson, a well-to-do Presbyterian engaged in commerce. Willie was studying to become a minister, and his eldest sister, Charlotte Higginson, was one of the first women in Ireland to attend university.

In 1906, RHB became assistant minister in Townsend Street Presbyterian Church in Belfast where the Higginson family worshipped. John Higginson was the superintendent of the Sunday School. I fancy I can see the Higginson girls, dressed in high-collared Edwardian frocks, sitting in a line in their pew at the Sunday morning service, listening attentively to the engaging young assistant minister with the country accent. Sitting beside Charlotte, and next to her brother Willie, was their sister Annie.

Annie Higginson – AHB

Annie was the one with the looks, according to Uncle Robin. RHB and Annie met in 1909, the year he first went to India, but they did not marry until 1915. By this time the First World War had begun and German U-boats were attacking British shipping. Annie took the last boat that was allowed to leave England with civilians aboard, and travelled to India, with her brother Willie as chaperon.

My mother said that RHB had to propose to AHB several times – until in 1913, when he was invalided back to Ireland, she finally said yes. Why did it take so long for her to accept his proposal?

My mother had a compelling way of telling family stories. She also took on a serious air when she read tea leaves to tell fortunes, so I'm not sure how reliable her stories really were. Anyway, she used to say that RHB was not considered good enough to marry her mother, because she came from a more important family than his.

RHB's obituary says, "His wife is a daughter of the late Mr John Higginson, linen merchant, Belfast." Ulster is proud of its noble linen industry. But when I checked with Uncle Robin and Uncle Billy, I discovered that John Higginson was a buyer and seller of cotton, a less distinguished fabric than linen. Be that as it may, the Higginsons come from a long-established family that can trace its roots in Ireland back to the early seventeenth century when Col Edward Higginson married Mary Savage of the Ards. The Savages go back even further, to the Anglo-Normans who arrived in the north of Ireland in the twelfth century.

Annie was one of eight children. Her father was killed by a tram in 1910 at the age of fifty-six. This tragedy greatly affected his family, changing the destiny of the children. Willie had to give up thoughts of becoming a minister and began to work in the family firm. Annie, who had trained as a teacher, also had to decide on her future.

Perhaps Willie Higginson had a role in Annie's decision to marry RHB. RHB's book *Through Gates of Hope*, published in 1947, is dedicated "to the memory of a friend, William Higginson".

There are several photographs of the wedding of RHB and AHB in India on 7th January 1915. RHB is dressed in clerical collar and dark frock coat. In one picture he has put one foot forward in a well-polished brogue. Is he holding Annie's hand behind her bouquet? Annie is dressed in white, her veil thrown back to reveal her dark hair. She smiles demurely. In another picture RHB and AHB stand on steps, while behind them, posing for posterity, are various clerics, one with a magnificent foot-long white beard, and six ladies in long dresses wearing wide Mary Poppins hats.

The family criticised RHB for not mentioning his wife in his memoirs. However, the memoirs are mainly about RHB's younger days, before he met AHB. She does appear in 1936 alongside RHB in his letters from around the world. RHB shows great admiration and affection towards her. RHB also dedicates several of his books to her. *Village Folk of India* (1924) is dedicated to "The sharer of my happiest experiences in India". My copy of *Waymakers in Manchuria* (1940) has an inscription in ink, "To you from me". My copy of *The Path of Valour* (1943) is inscribed to "Annie, with dearest love". *Fuller Life* (1947) has an ink inscription: "To the best beloved and only permanent member of the team. Robert Boyd". *A Garland of Memories* (1953) is dedicated simply "To my wife".

One of my mother's stories was about "the ring". Sometime in the 1920s, when RHB and Annie had returned from India, they were down on the family farm, in County Armagh, helping out at the haymaking, when Annie lost her wedding ring. According to my mother RHB took the haystack apart, straw by straw, working deep into the evening, until he found the ring. Perhaps "finding a needle in a haystack" would be more difficult, but still the story of RHB's single-mindedness stuck and was often retold. A hundred years later we still have the ring.

Those early wedding pictures confirm how good-looking Annie was when she was married. She appears as tall as RHB, with her long dark hair parted in the centre, and then drawn back on the sides and tucked under her veil. She has strong regular features, but also exudes a dreamy, pre-Raphaelite expression.

My memories of Annie Boyd are from forty-five years later, when we knew her as Gran.

On Belfast Sunday afternoons my brother and I would walk to where Gran lived in Sans Souci Park, across the Malone Road. We can't have been more than eight and nine years old, yet we were allowed to walk the distance of half a mile together by ourselves.

Gran would play the piano – stirring missionary hymns. Her favourite was "Onward Christian soldiers, marching as to war". We sometimes played up, stomping our feet and laughing while we marched around the piano. Gran frowned on this, expecting us to be serious soldiers. Later in the afternoon we would have toasted muffins by the fire, and Gran would take down RHB's book, *The Path of Valour*. She would read the inscription, "To Honor, Robin and Billy in proud happy and grateful memory of their gallant brother Jack", and the beginning of the chapter in which RHB writes about Jack, who was killed in Burma in the Second World War.

When we visited Gran soon after RHB's death, she was staying with a friend, Miss Hamill. I remember sunny afternoons in the garden and Gran naming the flowers. One of her favourites was Sweet William. I have also a fleeting memory of a little girl wearing a frock who peered into the garden from next door.

Later Miss Hamill was unwell and Gran came to live with us in Windsor Manse. There was plenty of space for her and her belongings as the Manse had seventeen rooms. Gran occupied the downstairs dining room and an upstairs bedroom. The "telephone room" (one room was dedicated solely to the black rotary telephone) was converted into a small kitchen, renamed "Gran's pantry".

One day Gran took John and me on the train from Adelaide station to Dunmurry, about five miles away. This was the village where she had grown up. We got off there, went under the bridge, and took the next train home.

When Gran was too ill to leave her downstairs room, I would lower puppets on strings from the window of my bedroom above to try to amuse her. She was usually dressed in dark clothes. Towards the end she began to lose her memory and thought my mother was hiding things from her. AHB lived in Windsor Manse until the last few weeks of her life and died on 27th February 1964.

I remember Gran's funeral. At the end the organ played Elgar's Enigma Variation, "Nimrod". It's a nostalgic Edwardian piece of music, flowing with sadness and melancholy. When I hear it I'm once again in Windsor, five pews from the back on the right side, watching AHB's coffin being borne out of the church.

For a long time I had little idea of what AHB was like when she was younger. However, my mother gave me a handwritten diary that AHB wrote in 1908, a year before she met RHB. It's a notebook of about twenty-five pages entitled *My first visit to London 24th Sept to 29th Sept 1908*. She was with her brother Willie Higginson.

I have tried to analyse Gran's writing to discover more about her young personality. She starts off writing beautifully, but does not keep this up. There is a flowery *f*. According to one graphology book this is a sign of culture. She often crosses her *t*s across a whole word. In the word *street* the two *t*s are crossed with a single stroke, and in *battle* the *l* is also crossed. According to the book this is a sign of "fondness for solving problems, braininess, excess of logicality". She was twenty-one.

The notebook starts:

> *It has always been the dream of my life – to see London; to walk its streets, to visit its sights, to hear its noise and to behold its wondrous river – in short to get close to the heart of that big throbbing city.*

As AHB leaves Belfast on board the ship, she writes:

> *What impressed me most I think was the work going on in the shipyards – we could hear the clanging noises of hammers on iron and steel – some large vessel was in building – slowly growing under men's hands, one day to sail far away and bear men to other lands.*

Perhaps the ship was the *Titanic*, the "unsinkable" liner that bore men, women and children to the bottom of the Atlantic Ocean on its maiden voyage in 1912.

In 1909 Annie reached London, the day after leaving Belfast.

> *About 1130 we neared London and soon we were seated in a hansom driving to the Hotel from Euston Station.*

She stayed in a hotel in Ludgate Hill and was impressed by the hustle and bustle of the great city. They went along Fleet Street:

... famous in history past and present. We saw the offices and premises of nearly all the newspapers, and here too the never-ending traffic was in full sway. A lady suffragette was marching courageously along selling her "votes for women" and followed by a mirthful crowd of spectators.

When I discussed the first draft of this story with Uncle Robin, he told me that nowadays people want to know more about missionaries' wives. Their story has seldom been told. He let me see some papers kept in a cardboard box. These included another diary of AHB's, this one from 1912, as well as letters of condolence written when she died in 1964.

The 1912 diary has a preface added by AHB many years later, in 1958. This was a few months after RHB died and one of her granddaughters, my sister Anne-Louise, was born:

March 1958

I meant to burn this girlish record – and yet, I didn't, for maybe someday one of my granddaughters may be helped by it. The woman of today looks back on her experiences and feels how little she has changed in her habit of thinking over the day's failures and being sorry for the same bad qualities still! But I would be quieter now. For now I realise the best thing is to look not inward to my sins, but upward to Jesus Christ and His glorious light and love and power and grace. I would give myself and my sins to Him and forget them and rejoice in His presence and love and

> power. How I thank Him that He led me to Rob and to India and to our happy life together! How He has guided and kept us through the years, and my prayers go forward to our children and grandchildren.

The diary that AHB saved from the fire shows that she deeply missed her father, killed two years before, and how devout she was.

> *A wakeful night. I could not sleep. The yearning for Father became intolerable. About one o'clock I arose and looked out to the quiet trees and fields. I opened the "daylight" and found the text for today "God shall wipe away all tears" etc. It came just like a direct message from God and I found a measure of peace. Although all day was a battle with tears I know He was near me.*

AHB enjoyed being a Sunday school teacher. She was unsure what to do with her life, and hints that she has to choose between love and companionship. There is no mention of RHB, but on one page she writes "a letter arrived today from India!"

After AHB's death in 1964, Grace Faris, one-time headmistress of Victoria College, a leading girls' grammar school in Belfast, wrote to my mother:

> *Dear Honor,*
> *The news of your mother's death filled me with sorrow. I appreciated her friendship and have always had a real admiration and affection for her.*

I never forgot the deep impression she made on me when, over fifty years ago, she addressed the Mission Conference during Assembly Week in May Street Church just before she went out to India as a young missionary. Her speech was inspired and her whole personality was in keeping. Her life of service bore out the promise she gave then. Now she has gone to the rest she has deserved and I am among the many who grieve her loss.

Yours affectionately,
Grace Faris

PART TWO
1909-1953

The Ambivalent Imperialist

After I had found about his early years, I set out to learn more about RHB's later life by reading his books. RHB wrote to persuade Christian folk, mainly in Ireland, but also in Britain, to support the Foreign Mission. His early books are quite dogmatic, but the longer he stays in India the more his writing becomes tolerant. This change is most marked in Village Folk of India, *published in 1924, the same year as E.M. Forster's* A Passage to India, *a novel about the changing relationship between Britain and India.*

The leading figure in India at that time, and one of the most significant leaders of the twentieth century, was "Mahatma" Gandhi. Gandhi was from Gujarat where RHB was based and they first met when "the Great Soul" was just beginning to become famous.

RHB talks about Gandhi in his books, at times in terms of admiration and at times more critically.

RHB wrote his books between 1909 and 1953, a period of massive upheaval in the world – including two World Wars, the demise of several Empires, among them the British Empire, with the independence and partition of Ireland and India. In 1957, the year RHB died, Ghana became the first British colony in Africa to achieve independence, and the Treaty of Rome setting up the EEC was signed. Britain's place in the world would never be the same again.

RHB's books can still be found in homes and libraries in Northern Ireland, and were recently rediscovered by a researcher, Justin Livingstone, who wrote a study entitled Ambivalent Imperialism: The Missionary Rhetoric of Robert Boyd.

The Lonely Road

RHB wrote his first book, *Manchuria and Our Mission There*, in 1908. It is introduced by Rev John Irwin, Joint Convener for Foreign Missions. Irwin, then the minister of Windsor Presbyterian Church, sets out the case for the mission:

> *For Christian people, their Lord's own command furnishes the supreme missionary motive. At the same time it is well to bear in mind that modern missionary enterprise followed in the wake of discovery and exploration – that it was when travel had been made comparatively easy, and men began to go to and fro and gain knowledge of their fellow-men throughout all the world, that sympathy was stirred and a great yearning came into the hearts of Christians for the salvation of the heathen.*

Dr Irwin adds:

> ... travel is still expensive; books are cheap; and it is from books mainly that we must be content to gather our knowledge of the people among whom our Church's agents labour.

This was in the days before movies, radio or TV. RHB's first book was written from research and from conversations with returned missionaries, but without any first-hand knowledge of Manchuria, part of China. It was only many years later, in 1936, that he visited the country.

Manchuria and Our Mission There is a short description of the country, the people and their different religions. RHB talks about the physical qualities and intellectual traits of Manchus and Chinese. He condemns the opium habit as one of the "vices" of the Chinese. He does not mention any outside responsibility for this vice, or the fact that Britain waged two wars against China in the 1860s in order to impose the opium trade on the country! RHB criticises the different religions in Manchuria. Confucianism has "failed" and Buddhism is "insufficient". Religions other than Christianity are all "hopeless".

In 1867, just a few years after the end of the Second Opium War, the Presbyterian Church in Ireland decided to send two missionaries to China. RHB tells the story of these pioneers, and their successors, and sets out the needs and opportunities to convert the people of Manchuria to Christianity.

Today people may find the idea of seeking to convert others to a new religion misguided. However, RHB's first book leaves no doubt of his purpose. Soon after writing his "mission statement" RHB set off to the mission field himself. He was supposed to go to Manchuria but was diverted instead to India.

By the time RHB wrote his second book called *Under the Banyan Tree* in 1913 he had lived and worked for four years in India. His third book, entitled *The Lonely Road*, was published in Fleet Street in 1919 with a price of 1s 9d, and has a summary on the front cover:

> *The author has spent ten years in India and has felt its subtle spell. He has also come into close contact with the silent masses, and his heart has been stirred by their poverty, their ignorance, their suffering and their superstition. Their hidden aspirations have perhaps appealed to him most, and the chapters on The Lonely Road – an incident of missionary life for which the book takes its title – and The Undying Quest, a sympathetic interpretation of the* Bhagavad Gita, *are unique.*

The Lonely Road was published when RHB was on furlough in Ireland. This was just after the First World War and the country was in turmoil. After the 1916 Easter Rising Britain tried to retain control in Ireland, but the country was divided between the mainly Catholic south, wanting independence, and the largely Protestant north wanting to remain part of the United Kingdom.

In the last chapter of *The Lonely Road* RHB writes:

> *The world war shook the foundations of most things.*

Perhaps it was too early for RHB to realise how much was about to change, but he already hints at what is to come.

> *At the call of the Empire's need her sons came flocking in thousands from afar, and it was only when men of all nations and colours and creeds stood side by side and fought shoulder to shoulder that the enemy of civilisation was vanquished. The war was won by brothers in arms.*

When I was at school we studied the many different causes of the First World War. However, RHB, writing immediately afterwards, has no doubts about who was responsible and who ought to be rewarded. He records that a total of 983,000 Indians served overseas, of whom 36,696 died.

> *As British citizens we owe India a debt which we can only repay in one way.*

RHB is deeply concerned about the "poverty, ignorance and suffering" of India, and makes a plea for more missionaries to be sent to India, "for His sake and out of gratitude for all that India did to help us win the war".

RHB also compares the time of tumult in India with events in Ireland.

> *For some strange reason the political agitators of India have adopted the phraseology and, to some extent, the methods of the agitator in Ireland. The two countries have at least this much in common, that religion lies at the root of their troubles.*

We do not learn what RHB thinks about constitutional change in Ireland, but he is in favour of gradual change in India. He refers to the "King Emperor" who has given "his royal sanction to a measure of self-determination for India. India is about to advance upon the road to the progressive realisation of responsible government."

The German, Austro-Hungarian, and Russian Empires all fell during the First World War, and the Ottoman Empire soon after. It was also seen as the turning point leading to the eventual demise of the British Empire.

In 1919 an event occurred in India that radically changed the views of leading Indians, among them Mahatma Gandhi and the Nobel Prize-winning poet Rabindranath Tagore, about the nature of British rule. This was the Amritsar massacre, when General Dyer ordered his soldiers to open fire on a group of people who were celebrating a religious festival. Dyer's troops killed or injured more than 2,000 innocent men, women and children.

The first time I visited India, in 2008, I took the train from New Delhi to Amritsar to visit the Sikhs' Golden Temple. However, my guide, Mr Singh, having put a pink turban around my head, took me first on his motorbike to see the place of the massacre, which at the time I only vaguely knew about. The place was a garden, called Jallianwala Bagh, which was a narrow piece of ground, walled on all sides, with no escape. To avoid the bullets many people leapt to their deaths into a well. I felt sad and angry as I imagined the cruel bloodbath that Dyer inflicted on civilians in that place.

As a young man Gandhi greatly admired Britain, but after the First World War he became disillusioned by the failure to reward India for its contribution to the war effort by honouring the commitment to greater Indian autonomy. When details of the Amritsar massacre emerged Gandhi was appalled and he began to press for an end to British rule. Tagore handed back his knighthood in protest. This was one of the most monstrous events in the history of the British Empire and a tipping point in British rule in India.

What did RHB think of Amritsar? Uncle Robin told me that RHB referred to that "damned man Dyer". He also told me that RHB remembered a shocking incident he saw, when he first arrived in India, of a British soldier beating an Indian in the street.

In *The Lonely Road*, published when he was forty years old, RHB remains convinced of the civilising mission of Empire, and the superiority of the Christian religion. The main message of the book is:

> ... the best gift we can bestow is an abundant and unfailing supply of men and women who are willing to spend their lives in the noble task of setting Jesus Christ forth... as the final goal of human life, its truest inspiration, its all-sufficient dynamic, and its complete satisfaction.

However, in this book RHB's love of India is as striking as his prescription to solve what he sees as the problems of India. RHB is passionate about the people, their plight, and the search for truth.

> When due weight has been given to all the adverse circumstances under which most foreigners live and

> work, India still possesses a most wonderful charm, and has a strange power of casting a spell over those who are in sympathy with her people, and have acquired by a knowledge of their language, customs and religion the magic key that unlocks their hearts.

Unlike many British officials RHB didn't just speak a few words of the local language. He became an expert in Gujarati, able to preach in the language, and remember it many years later.

RHB describes the wildlife found in the Indian village:

> ... its mischievous monkeys and impudent little squirrels; the shy mongoose, and the slinking jackal that makes the night resound with its plaintive barking; the gaudy-coloured screeching paroquet, the golden oriole, flashing like a sunbeam among the trees, the stately peacock that struts by the village floor, the restless flycatcher, the sweet-voiced magpie robin, the meditative kingfisher and the honey bird.

RHB contrasts this bucolic scene with the wretched poverty of the people. For this he blames the land tenure system. He describes the sickness, illiteracy and ignorance of the poor and how they often fall into the trap of moneylenders.

> ... One of the most urgent needs is a great forward movement in improved and extended primary education.

RHB believed that education should be practical, and he recommends that the teaching of agriculture should occupy a large place in village life.

RHB records how over 800,000 people died from the Plague in 1918 and how the world outbreak of influenza in that year killed six million Indians:

> *The whole situation is unspeakably sad.*
>
> *The problem of India is not merely one of education, economics and sanitation. The deepest needs of India are spiritual.*

So begins the chapter called "The Undying Quest", remarkable for its sympathetic study of the holy Hindu book, the *Bhagavad Gita*. RHB had been studying the *Bhagavad Gita* at the source:

> *One of the present writer's pandits has been giving his spare time to a poetic rendering of it in the vernacular, while another spends an hour each day reading and meditating upon it.*

RHB sets out the main argument of the *Gita* and talks of the caste system:

> *Caste has proved itself to be a yoke of bondage to the people of India and it is today one of the most baneful causes of poverty, ignorance and stagnation.*

However, RHB finds much of value in the doctrine of the *Gita*:

> ...This testimony to a personal and loving God to whom we can turn in times of doubt and difficulty, to personal immortality in or with God, to a means of salvation that is possible and open to all, and to the dedication of all the powers of our being to the service of God, is a wonderful monument of God's grace that stands unmoved and immovable amid all the rubbish heaps and ruins of time.

After acknowledging the value of the other religion, RHB reminds the reader of the superiority of Christianity:

> What in the Gita is only partial and obscure is in the New Testament full and clear.

And we come to the incident that gave the book its title. RHB recalls visiting a distant village, and remembers his conversation with an old man who listened to the missionary story, and who agreed in the duty of worshipping "the One Supreme Spirit", but who could not forsake the beliefs of his village.

> With all the dignity of a born courtier he bade us goodbye, and with all the warmth of a personal friend he pressed upon us the invitation to come back soon. As he turned to go away he lifted his hands to bestow upon us a benediction, and then by a graceful gesture he took all our sorrows and woes upon his own head, and symbolically at least and in intention I am sure bore them for us.

RHB finds this meeting very sad, and sadder two years later when he learns that the old man has died:

> ... *without the knowledge of the Saviour of mankind and without the inspiration and comfort that such knowledge brings. In the hour of death he was alone, and he was not cheered by the Christian hope of personal immortality and of a dateless life in the presence of God.*

The old man made a lasting impression on RHB. Many years later he came back to the story in *Through Gates of Hope* (1947).

By the time of *The Lonely Road* RHB's youthful certainty had become tempered by experience. I wonder if the title refers only to the road of the Hindu, uncomforted by hope in a Christian saviour. Perhaps RHB also had in mind the road of the missionary, faithfully trudging along, under the hot sun, to a small village, there to set up his stall, preach and sing, and attempt to convert "the heathen".

Village Folk of India

In April 1924 the United Council for Missionary Education in London published a new book by RHB called *Village Folk of India*. The author was then Convener of Foreign Mission, Presbyterian Church in Ireland. RHB had returned to Ireland in 1922, and was the full-time organiser of the Foreign Mission, based in Church House, Belfast.

Village Folk of India is dedicated to "the sharer of my happiest experiences in India". This must mean AHB. The book has a green linen cover, a frontispiece showing coconut trees, and is illustrated with some photographs.

Since the publication of *The Lonely Road* my mother had been born, in 1921. Ireland was divided that year, but RHB doesn't mention it. In India Gandhi had stepped up his campaign for self-rule.

The aim of the book is "to interest and instruct those who have not read much about India and are just beginning their study". It is designed for future missionaries. I wonder how many young men and women were inspired to become missionaries after reading it. Perhaps Uncle Robin was one. He was born in May 1924 and went to India as a missionary thirty years later.

Village Folk of India opens lyrically, with a country walk.

Morning, and the magpie robin sings as sweetly and merrily as ever robin sang. Other members of the feathered choir join in the chorus. They greatly err who say Indian birds are songless. Let them rise a little earlier in the morning and learn the truth for themselves.

RHB did not have much time for laziness.

RHB returns to the themes of *The Lonely Road*: the overwhelming poverty of India and its causes; the inequality of the caste system; the need for education, and for better agriculture.

He also makes a strong case for introducing cooperative banks. He would have been delighted to learn, as I found out on my visit there in 2012, that Anand, where he first worked, is now the centre of one of the largest and most successful cooperatives in India. The Amul dairy is today known for its products throughout the country. Amul started off as a spinoff from an EU-funded food aid project in the 1970s.

RHB writes:

One of the worst evils resulting from their poverty is the hopeless condition of debt into which many families fall. There are millions in India who are paying, or trying to pay, interest on the debt contracted by their fathers or grandfathers, with no hope of ever getting free, and with no ambition to become independent. Among the outcastes and aborigines particularly the dire poverty often leads a man to mortgage his services as a labourer, or even those of his children. From this condition, which is virtually that of slavery, they have little chance of ever freeing themselves.

When I first read this passage I wondered what RHB would think of the modern day microfinance movement, as pioneered most famously by Bangladeshi Muhammad Yunus, founder of the Grameen Bank.

RHB continues:

The Village Bank lends at from nine to twelve per cent on security, and as a rule, the necessary guarantors see that the loans are paid on the appointed date. One of the best things about the Cooperative movement is the special effort it makes to set people free from the serfdom of debt. As a rule, only small sums are lent, and for short periods, but in order to clear off an old debt a larger sum can be borrowed for a longer period. It is a great day in a man's life when for the first time he has shaken himself free of the fetters of inherited indebtedness, and steps forth a liberated man.

I met Muhammad Yunus several times during my four years in Bangladesh. He is one of the best-known Bangladeshis, and the winner of the Nobel Prize for his work on microcredit and microfinance. He has also pioneered the concept of "social business". He is a smiling, direct and intelligent man, a charismatic figure and an inspiration to millions of people around the world. The repayment rate of his bank, which lends to the poorest, is much better than that of commercial banks. It is a system that has been copied all over the world. In Bangladesh other approaches to helping the poorest people have been pioneered by BRAC, an organisation founded by the late Sir Fazle Abed. I was often impressed by how BRAC's work brought together applied research and agricultural extension at low cost and with great benefits to the poorest people. For example, BRAC has pioneered new varieties of rice that are resistant to salt water and adapt to the effects of climate change. I'm sure RHB, son of a poor County Armagh farmer, would approve of all these new ways of helping the poorest farmers in Asia.

Mahatma Gandhi
The Great Soul

Mahatma Gandhi appears in the first chapter of *Village Folk of India*. In a lively prologue RHB imagines old men in the village discussing the latest news. One says:

> *Oh, everybody is talking about the elections. They say the swarajists (home rulers) have won, and that they are going to put a stop to Government. Mahatma Gandhi will soon be released from prison, and the tax on salt will be withdrawn.*

One of Gandhi's most famous protests was against the salt tax. In 1930 Gandhi marched many miles to the sea. He collected salt in his hands and laid it down on the sand. He did this to provoke the colonial authorities. They locked him up for not respecting the state monopoly on salt.

In his book RHB introduces another old man who is more sceptical:

True, there is nothing but revolution these days. But what good will come of it all? Peace is best. That is my opinion.

A few pages later RHB writes:

One of the commonest sounds in the village is that of the loom. The cloth they weave is for the most part coarse, and was up until recently worn chiefly by those engaged in rough work. Mr Gandhi's movement has increased its popularity, and it is not unusual to see educated gentlemen clad in coarse homespun.

The Gandhi we encounter in these pages is not just a figure RHB had read about in the papers. When I visited Gandhi's ashram in 2012 I remembered that my mother had told me that her father had met Gandhi. So when I returned from Gujarat, I asked Uncle Robin to tell me more. His answer took me aback.

'Well, RHB met Gandhi twice. The first time was in Anand in 1915. Gandhi was still acting as a lawyer, and they shared the same platform.'

'What platform was that?' I asked. I was thinking of Uncle Robin's great love of trains, and now had a picture in my mind of Gandhi in white cloth beside RHB in his clerical collar, a pair of figures in a Merchant Ivory film emerging from behind the steam of a locomotive.

'Well, actually they were both recruiting for soldiers to fight in the First World War. My father was awarded a medal for his efforts, and Gandhi – it was only later that he became a pacifist.'

'And the other time?' I asked. 'Oh, that was at the ashram,' said Uncle Robin. 'They sang hymns together. One was "When I survey the wondrous cross". Gandhi loved that hymn.'

Much changed in the years after the Great War. By the time of *Village Folk in India* the British government had failed to live up to its promises of granting greater freedom to India in recognition of India's war contribution. A disillusioned Gandhi had abandoned his faith in the British Empire, no longer dressed himself in European clothes, and was urging Hindus to boycott British goods and to spin their own cloth.

In the chapter "The tide from the West", RHB devotes three pages to Gandhi. RHB says that at the end of the Great War, "the idea of self-determination was on all men's lips". Woodrow Wilson, the US President, a Presbyterian of Scotch-Irish descent, and one time President of Princeton University where RHB studied, had made this concept a central idea in the post-war settlement. RHB describes how "A great tidal wave of nationalism swept over India." The Nationalist movement had begun to touch the villages and he talks of "the wonderful nationalist leader Mr Gandhi, popularly known as 'Mahatma' or 'Great Spirit'". He describes him as "remarkable… filled with a burning passion for the rights of his fellow countrymen". He is "single minded and a man of high ideals with an unconcealed reverence for Jesus Christ and his teaching". Nevertheless Gandhi "does not know human nature with its warring passions, and his political speeches at a critical time played upon the passions of men who had not the same discipline and self-restraint he possesses. Non-violent non-cooperation failed, and its use ended in violence and bloodshed."

RHB remains sympathetic to the Government "which was compelled to restrain him":

> *As a political leader Mr Gandhi failed, but the faith of the masses of India in him as an ideal saint has never been shaken, and now that he is at liberty again, it is hoped by many that, freed from political entanglement and with eyes open to the spiritual condition of his fellow countrymen he may yet lead them to something greater and better than they have as a people aspired to.*

Village Folk of India is the most political of RHB's books, remarkable for the assessment of Gandhi – admiration for the spiritual leader, mixed with a dim view of his political skills. RHB explains more about his encounters with Gandhi in his memoir, *While I Remember*:

> *My first glimpse of Mahatma Gandhi was at Gondal railway station in Kathiawar. He had recently come home from South Africa, and in his native province many of his admirers gave him a welcome and listened to his story with rapt attention. On that occasion he was scantily dressed, with a blanket thrown over his shoulder. He was only at the beginning of his career then, and people outside the circle of admirers looked*

at him with curiosity rather than the reverence that was to come.

My next contact with him was at Nadiad, one of the busiest and most politically-minded centres of Gujarat. It was during the First World War, at a meeting convened by government officials in support of a recruiting campaign for the labour corps. I was there because the young men of our Farm Colonies had been among the first to volunteer for Mesopotamia, and had set an example to other communities. Among the speakers of the day was a Christian farmer who had returned safely, and had a rousing story to tell of the conditions of life over there in health and in sickness. He had not been overworked, the food was good, medical attention was excellent, and the pay was regular. There was only one drawback: the sound of a whistle had to be obeyed, morning, noon and night!

Other speakers had their turn, and then the chairman requested Mr Gandhi to say a few words. He was fully dressed that day as a Kathiawari gentleman. On his head was a large pagadi, neatly folded. His dhoti touched his ankles, and his scarf hung loosely around his neck, and fell to his knees. He wore country shoes. At first he spoke in Gujarati, slowly and in quiet tones, as if he were addressing an individual and not an assembly. After a while he said that he could express his thoughts better in English, and he continued in that language. He didn't say much about the war, but he laid great stress on British justice, declaring his conviction if the British thought he was the right man to be made Viceroy of India they would without discrimination or hesitation appoint him. The speech was difficult to follow, and its impression was vague, but a gentleman who thanked him won applause when he stated that Mr Gandhi was a person who was "filled with electric power".

Several years passed before I had the pleasure of meeting the Mahatma again. We were stationed in Ahmedabad at that time. Mr R.T. Archibald, the missionary of the C.S.S.M. was eager to meet him, or at least to visit the ashram on the banks of the Sabarmati where he lived. We went out one evening, and were shown round the spinning and weaving sheds and the model farm. By that time the sun was setting and it was time for evening worship. On a raised platform rugs were spread and pillows set. The inmates of the ashram assembled and after a while the Mahatma, scantily dressed, came out and sat in the place prepared for him. Some young people sang hymns addressed to Rama and Sita, and others played Indian instruments. The Mahatma entered into the spirit of the songs.

When the singing was ended he beckoned to us to come forward. He welcomed us most cordially, and engaged in conversation, especially about the spinning and weaving, and the use for such home industries in the Indian villages. He asked us to sing some English hymns, and sent an attendant to bring hymn books from the house. Two of the hymns he chose were "We shall know each other better when the mists have rolled away" and "When I survey the wondrous cross".

Before leaving one of us ventured to ask him how he could at the same time appreciate "When I survey

> the wondrous cross" and the hymns in honour of Rama and Sita which the young people were singing. His reply was that to a person like him Rama and Sita were only names, but to these children who had been taught to adore them they were life, and it would be wrong for him to undermine their simple beliefs or destroy their childlike faith. To that extent he carried his doctrine of non-violence.

What did RHB mean by this last sentence? In the handwritten manuscript he added one more sentence: "That was the extent to which he carried the doctrine of non-violence. Better allow people to enjoy the illusion of falsehood than cause them the pain of discovering the truth!"

However, RHB, writing at the end of his life, crossed out that last thought.

What did Mahatma Gandhi mean by his answer? In 2012, when I visited the ashram. I was struck by a series of stone tablets setting down the philosophy of the ashram. One of them is about "Equality of Religions":

> The ashram believes that the principal faiths of the world constitute a revelation of truth but as they have all been outlined by imperfect man they have been affected by imperfections and alloyed with untruth. One must therefore entertain the same respect for the religious faiths of others as one accords to one's own.

The Prevailing Word

Published in 1953, when RHB was seventy-three, *The Prevailing Word* is RHB's last book, based on notes "pigeon-holed" during the preparation of *Couriers of the Dawn*, which was published for the centenary of the Irish Presbyterian Mission in 1940. The book shows the development of the mission stations and the evolution of missionary methods. It is a history of missionaries in Gujarat. Uncle Robin's later history of the Presbyterian Church in India takes up the story, in a more systematic and detailed way.

The Prevailing Word is a tale of "the seed being sown", but with a harvest of few converts, for the stigma of conversion was very great. In a postscript RHB explains that the word "prevailed" does not mean that all became Christians, simply that "in conflict with various forms of evil, the Gospel proved its power to overcome". Moslems,

Brahmins and outcastes were converted, if they believed. "The Word cannot prevail unless it is believed. It cannot be believed until it is heard, and it cannot be heard without heralds who proclaim it."

For the first time in RHB's published books there are elements of doubt, of explanation, and of criticism. There were many hindrances to acceptation of the Word.

The first difficulty was in the nature of the message.

"We preach Jesus Christ as Lord of all." This message was not toned down. RHB says that Indians already placed Christ alongside Krishna, Gautama, Gandhi, but "… we cannot lower His claim or His right".

"We preach that all who are in Jesus Christ are one." There is no caste system in Christianity, and RHB thought that this may have prevented Indians from accepting the religion.

RHB says another obstacle to conversion was "Social Ostracism and Economic pressure", even persecution. Especially in the early days families often rejected their children if they converted to Christianity.

RHB also criticises lack of support from the home church in Ireland. "We ought to have had more men." "We have never had enough women missionaries." "Not enough was done to train young men."

A final problem brings us back to Gandhi, whom RHB simply refers to as "the most famous of Indians":

Misrepresentation of missionary methods and motives has also had a deterring effect on many or have so poisoned their minds that they could not bring themselves to the point of even enquiring what the message of the missionaries and their books is about. When a group of young men joined the Church in Rajkot, under the ministry of Rev H.R. Scott, reports were spread that they were forced into the breaking of caste by eating flesh and drinking liquor. That rumour was referred to without comment many years afterwards by the most famous of Indians, and it is still believed.

Scott was a close friend of RHB's and of Gandhi. In my last conversation with Uncle Robin, in May 2018, he showed me a photograph of the guests at RHB's marriage and pointed out Scott. He told me Scott wrote to Gandhi about the allegations that the missionaries had used dubious methods to convert people, and Gandhi replied to him, "About beef-eating and wine drinking at baptism I merely repeated what I had heard". However Gandhi did not publicly retract the story, as RHB would have wished. RHB and Uncle Robin were right to be concerned about the lasting damage Gandhi's criticism of missionaries would do. David Gilmour in his 2018 book *The British in India* repeats Gandhi's view.

Robert Boyd's Rhetoric Reviewed

In 2012, a few years after I had started this voyage, I discovered another fellow traveller, a stowaway on my boat. A researcher called Justin Livingstone had written an academic article about RHB. Like me he had recently been reading RHB's books, but with a more detached and critical eye. I found his paper online and read it with a mixture of excitement and alarm. Would he debunk my heroic grandfather, as the title suggested? Here are some extracts from the abstract of his work:

AMBIVALENT IMPERIALISM:
THE MISSIONARY RHETORIC OF ROBERT BOYD
by Justin Livingstone

Abstract

Postcolonial Studies has directed much of its critique of British Imperialism at those informal agents responsible for the cultural crimes of colonial exploitation.

Missionaries have routinely been charged with cultural annihilation and for conjuring up images of different and distant peoples and places. In keeping with a growing trend in historical studies, this article revisits the complexity of missionary involvement in colonialism, and its rhetorical construction of otherness. But I do this by examining as literature writings produced by missionaries themselves. Specifically, I analyse the works of Robert Boyd, a missionary in India in the early twentieth century and later Convener of Foreign Mission for the Presbyterian Church in Ireland... I argue that the relationship between mission and imperialism is one of ambivalence, an ever-complex dynamic, which refuses the cliché of the Bible and the gun as the dual tools of empire.

... At least since Edward Said's Orientalism *(1978), Literary Studies has contributed much by interrogating those western voices responsible for the rhetorical construction of "otherness" in binary opposition to western "Civilisation". One voice routinely condemned for its "othering" images and*

for perpetuating cultural annihilation, was that of missionaries. Their writings enjoyed remarkably large audiences and so their historical role in constituting the discourses of imperial power and in shaping British perceptions of different and distant peoples and places is undeniable. However, in contrast to the dismissive terms in which the relationship between missionaries and empire was originally discussed, historical scholarship in recent years has fruitfully revealed a much more subtle interplay of complexity and nuance.

Specifically, I will examine the works of missionary author, Rev Robert Boyd, who wrote prolifically from the early 1900s through to the 1950s… That Boyd was considered distinguished among missionaries, and among his peers in the Presbyterian Church, was illustrated in his election to the Moderatorship of the General Assembly in 1947.

His obituary in the Presbyterian Herald depicts his truly greatest achievement as the enhancement of "the literature of our mission". Boyd may well deserve this accolade, for his work is still drawn on as a source for the history of mission in both India and Manchuria. However, what is intriguing about Boyd's writing is that it fuses ethnography and geographical survey with detailed descriptions of evangelical endeavour. His pamphlet series, Trophies for the King, *sketches descriptions of converts won for the mission whilst another biographical series recounts the heroics of missionaries in the field. These sit alongside his brief ethnographic pen-portraits of*

> village life in both India and Manchuria. Through an analysis of Boyd's variegated output, I contend that the dynamic between Christianity and empire has been ever complex, and that missionary imperialism has always been fundamentally ambivalent.

The full text of Livingstone's article is available online. When I told Uncle Robin about the article he met the author and discussed his conclusions.

"Ambivalent", meaning to be "unsure, doubtful or indecisive", is not an adjective that I would associate with RHB. Was RHB an agent of imperialism? In one sense he was. He served and was rewarded by the British Empire for his efforts to persuade young Indians to take part in the First World War. But he was also enlightened by his direct experience of the suffering of the Indian people. He argued that India's contribution to the war effort should be rewarded and he favoured greater local democracy. RHB always showed great love for his fellow man and for humanity. In his view of the world duty and love were inseparably entwined. God and country went together, and there was no higher calling than sacrifice for both.

In 2018, on my last visit to Uncle Robin in Edinburgh, he showed me a faded mauve file containing thirty letters written by RHB to his children from his trip around the world in 1936–7. He asked me to look at these letters, and at some other papers, and see what might be published. I didn't find much in the other papers, but in the letters I discovered some of the finest of RHB's writing, perhaps with the exception of *The Path of Valour*, to which I return in Part IV. I also found an answer to a dilemma in my mind about how to be fair to RHB, who is unable to question my interpretations, and yet how to avoid being uncritical of him. What better way to resolve this problem than to allow RHB to speak for himself.

PART THREE

1936-1937

Letters from Around the World

In August 1936 RHB set out with AHB on a voyage around the world. They travelled across the Atlantic Ocean by boat, through Canada by train and across the Pacific Ocean to Japan. From there they went to Japanese-controlled Korea and Manchuria in China where, as Convenor of the Irish Presbyterian Foreign Mission, RHB paid an official visit. From China they went by boat to Singapore and Malaya and to India, where they revisited the places in Gujarat where RHB had served as a young missionary, where they started their married life, and where Jack and Honor were born. In February 1937 they returned home by boat, across the Indian Ocean and the Mediterranean Sea.

During their six-month tour RHB and AHB wrote many letters to their children. RHB gave instructions that his hand-written manuscripts should be kept together. In 2019 I typed out and shared the letters with RHB's descendants, sending them episodes each week over a few months. I made a few cuts here and there but sent them the bulk of the letters that are reproduced below.

Reading and transcribing these hand-written letters allowed me to get to know RHB in a new way. He wrote legibly which made my task a pleasure. (There may be some inconsistencies in spelling place names). He comes across as passionate and determined, as I already knew. But he is also funny and affectionate, in a way that I had before only suspected. Although I don't have my mother's letters to her father, many of his replies are addressed to her and remind me of her. He chose a pet name for her – Eyebright – after an Irish wildflower. Some answers to questions I wished to ask my grandfather come down through the eighty-three years since RHB wrote these letters. They also stirred memories that Uncle Billy had forgotten. To complete the picture I include some of Uncle Billy's own recollections of 1936 and 1937.

1936: What a year to set out on a journey around the world! The rise of the dictators threatened peace in Europe and the world. Nazi Germany reoccupied the Rhineland, violating the Treaty of Versailles that was the settlement after the First World War. Mussolini's fascist Italy annexed Ethiopia. In July the Spanish army of Africa launched a coup d'état against the Spanish Republic, beginning the Spanish

Civil War. Historians see this as a precursor of the Second World War, with one side supported by Nazi Germany and the other by Communist Russia. In August the Summer Olympics were held in Berlin, allowing Hitler to show the world the frightening might of the Third Reich.

The Berlin Olympics was the first live TV coverage of a sports event. The BBC started TV broadcasts later in the year, but TVs did not arrive in most British homes until the 1950s. The 1930s was a time before computers, before electric typewriters. People with urgent messages could send a telegram, but international phone calls were almost unheard of. Around the world people kept in touch by post, with long delays between sending a letter and receiving a reply. Travel by air was becoming more common, but planes were still a rare enough sight to be noted. In 1936 the first flight by the new Irish airline Aer Lingus took place. Most people travelled across the Atlantic by boat. The luxury ocean liner Queen Mary sailed on her maiden voyage across the Atlantic that year. It was from a less prestigious liner that RHB wrote his first letter, in pencil and in big letters to my mother, aged fifteen, back at home in Belfast.

Eyebright

1 *Duchess of York*
14/8/36

Dear Honor,

At last I know the name of the ship we are sailing on; it is the *Duchess of York*.

I came away without my fountain pen. If you see it in the study please keep it safe till I return. Do not let Tom, Dick and Harry use it!

I hope you will have a good time at the cottage and at other places and that you will be fit for school. We will remember you with all our love. No room for more except

Much love from Father

P.S. I hope you will be able to read this. If not I can write L A R G E R letters.

2

Claresholm,
Alberta
Canada
27/8/36

Dear Robin,

It is hard to believe that this is the same month as that in which we left home. It seems as if it ought to be a new year. We have travelled so far and have seen so much that I am beginning to be a bit confused.

We received great kindness from Mr and Mrs Armour and others in Toronto. It was very warm there, almost like India. We left on Sunday night at 10.40. Mr Armour was going to Ottawa by another train a little later and he saw us off. We had a section, that is a sort of little bedroom of our own. It cost more but it was worth having it. There were two berths, an upper and a lower, a wardrobe and a whole bedroom complete. We slept fairly well, but it was a bit hot. All the windows, double they are, were tightly closed, but there was a current of cool air, cooled by ice, coming in all the time. "Air conditioned" it is called.

When we got up in the morning we looked out upon lovely scenery, trees, rivers and lakes. It was like that all day. In the afternoon we went by the shores of Lake Superior. The scenery was grand, and looked like a hundred Lough Ernes. Lakes and islands, and islands and lakes. There were glorious wildflowers, pink and yellow, and shrubs with rich, red berries, also flaming rowan trees.

The curves on the line were very interesting. At the rear of the train there is a parlour car, and at the end of it there is a platform like a covered verandah. There is room for half a dozen or more chairs on it, and people sit out there in the open air looking at the view till the dust drives them in. From there and from the parlour or observation car, we could often see the engine away in front and a part of the train turning the corner around a bend of the lake. The train stopped at a number of stations, for ten or fifteen minutes, when everybody got out for a walk. At some of these stations the time was changed. For example we arrived in Fort William at 8.45 p.m., stayed for some time and left it at 9.35. Up till then we kept Eastern Time. After that we had central time. Then we came to Broadview at 4.10 p.m., remained a quarter of an hour and departed at 3.25, having changed from Central to Mountain Time. Since then we have kept M.T.

At Winnipeg we were met by the Secretary of the Bible Society who showed us the town and his offices. At Moose Jaw we had half an hour. My brother Joe was there from Crane Valley, sixty miles away. I sent him a telegram in the afternoon. He happened to be in the town when it arrived, and just as he was he got into a car coming to Moose Jaw, and so we met for the first time in thirty years.

We reached Calgary an hour late on Wednesday yesterday morning. That was the first time we were late since we left Toronto. We were up to time all the way till then. Mr Armour had sent word to the secretary of the Bible Society to meet us. He, poor man, was unable to do so, owing to the death of his wife, but three gentlemen were on the platform waiting for us, and they were full of kindness, brought all our luggage to the bus station and us to the Bible House, where others came to meet us and wish us God speed. At eleven we got one of the "Greyhound buses", which brought us to Claresholm at two o'clock. There we found Aunt Florence waiting for us. We are now at her house, ten miles from Claresholm, and in view of the foothills of the Rockies. She and her husband settled here a few years ago, and the seasons have been bad since then. The whole country is scorched like India and the wheat is very short. Much of it has no grain at all. The gardens have not been planted and the young trees are finding it hard to survive. There will be enough fodder to keep the cattle alive, but a good season and a full crop is greatly needed if the people here are to remain on the land at all. There are little animals called gophers in great abundance. In the distance they look like squirrels. There are coyotes which do a lot of harm to the flocks of chickens and turkeys. Not far from here there's a beavers' dam. We may see it before we leave.

Now the best of good wishes to you all. Share this letter with the others. The 1st of September will soon be here. We will be thinking about school. We both send our warmest love.

God bless you all
Dads

3

Deer Lodge
Lake Louise
Alberta
Grosvenor Hotel,
Vancouver B.C.
Sept 3rd 1936

Dear Honor,

    Although I am using this paper we are now in Vancouver. We arrived this morning at nine o'clock and the first race was to the office of the C.P.R. to look for letters. We got them and they gave us a real thrill of joy. First we read the postcard from you and Jack, and then we gloated over the letters from all of you. We have had nothing more delightful since we left home. Jack's letter will give you a good deal of the news up to yesterday morning. We left Lake Louise after one o'clock and we had a most wonderful day through the Rockies till eight when it grew dark. The mountains, glaciers, rivers, canyons were indescribable in majesty and grandeur. We saw so much that both our eyes and minds became tired and it really was restful when night drew its curtain round us.

    In the afternoon when we were sitting in the observation car, someone shouted "a bear" "a black bear". We looked out and down below us, in its nature haunt was a beautiful bear with a coat of glossy black, climbing over the rocks. It looked so well out in the wide woods and not cooped up in close quarters like those we saw in the National Park at Banff, where their quarters are not a bit better than those at Bellevue.

In the evening we arrived at a lovely place called Sicamous. The station and hotel are on the edge of a lake. Some people got out to stay there for the night. We had decided to go on, so we walked up and down the platform for fresh air and at the call "all aboard" got into the train for the night. We occupied an upper and a lower berth in a long carriage. Our beds were made up there and a curtain drawn across. There are two long rows of these sections in a carriage, with the corridor between.

We did not sleep very well, as there were many stops and much jolting, stopping and starting. I got up at six o'clock and Mother was up soon afterwards. We had fresh air through an open door, breakfast in the dining car, and punctually at nine o'clock the long journey from ocean to ocean came to an end.

Yesterday I saw in the paper that letters posted here today would catch the *Queen Mary* at New York, so I want this one to go by the record breaker. This place is all decorated for the "Show" and Jubilee celebrations. The red, white and blue bunting and the Union Jacks remind us of July in Belfast. We are to sail on Saturday and will look forward to the next letters at Yokohama; that will not be as long a wait as this was.

My dearest love to you. Last night I dreamed about you and I was calling you Speedwell and Eyebright as of old. Blessings on you.

Dad

P.S. Glad indeed to know the pen is safe. Keep it for me. There is none like it!

Canada to Japan

4

R.M.S. *Empress of Russia*
14th September 1936

Dear Honor,

It is years and years since we left home and it is hard to believe that we had letters from you all at Vancouver. Of course the last of them was written on the 18th or 19th of August, that is merely a month ago. We are thirsting for news and looking forward with a thrill to our letters on the 16th at Yokohama. That will not be long now.

This voyage has been very pleasant. The ship is not crowded as the *Duchess of York* was and we have got to know more people. Of course we have had a longer time together. We have a very fine cabin, with two large wardrobes and plenty of room for us and all our belongings. The routine of the day is much the same as it was on the other ship. At 7.15 the Chinese steward comes with tea, or orange juice, or biscuits, or whatever else we want, and then he asks: 'Bath for lady, bath for gentleman?' and we have our bath. Usually we are out for a walk on deck before 8.30. There has been a good deal of swell on the sea and many people have been absent, but on the whole the weather has been good, except that there has not been much sunshine.

We spend the morning sitting reading, walking or playing deck games and then we have lunch at one o'clock. There is afternoon tea at 4.30 and dinner is at 7.15. The stewards carry round soup and biscuits at eleven o'clock. They are just doing it now. I have only taken it once. It is the only thing I have missed! Mother has been quite a good sailor although she missed some meals in the dining rooms and lost!some more! Today she is perfectly well and enjoying everything.

The captain is a friend of Arthur McNeill's and lives beside him at Vancouver. We met his son there. He has been very kind to us and had us up in his room for tea. He asked me to take the service on the first Sunday. I read the prayers and he read the lesson. Yesterday I did the same and the Staff Captain read the lesson. I enjoyed the services. The hymns were well-known: "Rock of Ages", "The King of Love", "Jesus Lover" &c. We had Presbyterians, Baptists, Church of England, Quakers, Plymouth Brethren, and I don't know how many others present. Yesterday at five o'clock we had a second service. I was asked to take charge of it. Two Baptists and a Plymouth Brother (from Cork, but forty-two years in China) prayed. A United Church of

Canada Minister read the Chapter and I preached from the text: "I know whom I have believed." It was one of the most mixed congregations I ever saw. One of the priests (we have about a dozen of them as well as three nuns) remained in the saloon; stood up during the singing and listened to the sermon. We had "All People", "Rock of Ages", "The King of Love" and "Jesus Lover". There was an offering for Marine Charities, and we got a little over 12/6.

Since we left Vancouver we have put our watches back around fifty minutes a day, and then we dropped out the 11th of September. On Thursday there was a notice in the ship's News Sheet: "To-morrow will be Saturday". I was looking forward to this missed day, hoping that it would fall on the 10th so that I might be able to tell you that I had no birthday this year! But I was born a day too soon for that distinction. When I went down to breakfast on the 10th, I was the only person at the table. Mrs Kneckstal was poorly, so was Mrs Boyd and Dr Murray, and Mr Kneckstal had breakfast earlier with the baby. I found an extra Menu Card on the table with "Birthday Greetings" stamped across it. I wondered who had told the secret to the head steward, but I soon remembered that the place and date of my birth and even my age were all on the form that I had filled and handed to the purser after I came on board. In the evening when I went down to dinner we found an enormous cake on the table, with one huge red candle in the centre. The candle was lit afterwards and when coffee time came I cut the first slice and then the head steward cut slices for all those who were at dinner. Still there was some left and we had enough to give to all who were at tea the next afternoon. Two days later a lady at another table had a birthday also and she had a lovely cake too, but instead of one large candle she had a number – she knows how many – small ones like what we use at home. She and her party came late for dinner, but I had to see the steward about the Sunday afternoon service and while I was in the saloon I got a piece larger than my own! Then we all had a share at tea the next afternoon. So I have had four slices of birthday cake. Remember that for next year! The steward says there will be some more birthdays before the ship reaches Yokohama.

15/9/36

We are now going toward the south. The sea is calm. The port-holes are open. Most people are well and there is a general air of happiness. Tomorrow the captain and officers will likely put on their white uniforms, at least that is what some of them told me, and on Wednesday morning we will reach Yokohama from which this letter and others will be posted via Siberia. We will spend a few hours in Yokohama and then go on to Tokio. I'll not know our programme till I get letters. I would like to be in Seoul, Corea for Sunday, but that may not be possible as it might not give enough time for Tokio.

Now the rest of the letter, indeed the whole of it, if you will read between the lines, is just LOVE to you and Jack and Robin and Billy. Remember us to Dr Sara and Miss McElderry, Uncle Willie, Aunt Elma, John, Selina, the Aunties &c. I wonder how Mrs Crawford is. We often think of her. Give her our best wishes

Again, dear Honor, our love, Daddy

5

Moukden
Manchuria
26/9/36

Dear Honor,

As Jack will be away when this arrives, I am writing to you. You might send it on to him, as I have not time to write two letters of this length.

Where am I to begin? We posted our last letters on our arrival at Yokohama. We landed early in the morning. The secretary of the mission of the United Church of Canada had written to his missionaries in Japan asking them to arrange to have us met. So before we got into harbour Mr Albright was on board and was hurrying round asking for "Dr" Boyd. Up till then the prefix had been concealed, but thereafter everybody seemed to want to call me by that name! When we reached the dock we found that a Japanese gentleman, Mr Ebisawa, of the National Christian Council of Japan, to whom I had written from Belfast, was also there to meet me. He took charge of us, helped us through the customs, which was a very easy affair, and got the Yokohama Express to take charge of our baggage. We went to the C.P.R. office to look for more letters, as we had no news from Jack, Robin and Billy. There was nothing there, so I left our address at Moukden so that the letter might be sent on as soon as possible. Then we went to the station and out by electric car for half an hour to Tokio. Mr Ebisawa had arranged for us to stay with an American missionary called Hoekje, pronounced Hookye, we drove out there by taxi, a long way out in the suburbs of Tokio. It was lovely to get into a house again.

We were there in time for lunch, then after a rest we went with our host and hostess by street car and electric train to Kamakura, where there is an enormous image of Buddha over forty feet high, one of the sights of Japan. The journey out was our first glimpse of Japan and we enjoyed looking at the fields and trees and houses. The image of Buddha is in a nice little park with lovely trees. It is impressive in a sort of way, sitting there ever the same with downcast eyes, deep in meditation without thought, if you can understand what that is; but it seemed to me to be so cold and remote from life, and so uninterested in people and their joys and sorrows, that I could not rise to the heights of ecstasy to which the writers of guide-books had risen when they wrote their descriptions of its wondrous beauty.

We walked back to the railway station and had time to look at the shops and other things, all of which reminded us so much of India. A few purchases were made about which Mother can tell you more than I can – Japanese pictures and little boxes etc. When we returned to Tokio our host brought us to see the great central street where the large shops are. People love to walk there in the evenings to look at the windows and the shops erected on the footpath, and to see the thousands of electric signs of all shapes and colours that make the famous street look like fairy-land.

Next morning we were up early and I went to the college chapel in which over a thousand students had assembled for morning prayers. There I met a Japanese gentleman who had been to Jerusalem in 1928 and we had much in common. I was asked to address the boys and he translated for me. I will not trouble you with the address! It was thrilling to see all those boys. We did not go over the college building, but we saw many of the students doing their drill, which is compulsory, and is preparation for their military service which is part of the life of the Japanese.

Immediately after breakfast on Thursday I had to go to the city to meet Mr Ebisawa and get some business done. First we went to the bank where I got some Japanese money. Then we went to the government offices of various people to meet them and get introductions from them to similar people in Manchuria. That took a long time and it was very tiresome to me. Several times we drove past the gate of the Imperial Palace along by the moat which separates it from the city. After lunch we went to the tourist bureau and purchased tickets for Moukden and made other arrangements for the journey and last of all we called at the Y.M.C.A. to see the secretary. There we had a good deal of talk, which was helped by a welcome cup of tea. Before I left one of the gentlemen asked me about my passport and advised me to go to the Manchukuo embassy early next morning to get their stamp upon it. We thought it might save some trouble at the border.

That was a disappointing bit of business. Mother and I had arranged to go to Nikko – one of the great sights – in an early train. I had to give that up but hoped to go on the second one. I missed that one by five minutes, and so I missed Nikko altogether, to my great disappointment. I got the passport stamped however, and there was a little satisfaction in that, which almost vanished when I learnt that all that was necessary might have been done on the train at Autung!

Well, there I was stuck for a day. Mother and Mrs Hoekje later returned from Nikko, and that evening, after dinner, we started off on the train on the way to Manchuria.

We took a slow train that reached Kobe about seven in the morning, and allowed us to stay there for two or three hours to see it before going on to Shimonoseki. We sat up late hoping to see Fuji, but we were disappointed. It was a restless night. The train went through tunnel after tunnel and we were glad when morning came. The country was beautiful, real Japan, and we gazed and gazed at the hills, the woods, and the fields cultivated like well-kept gardens.

At Kobe station we were met by our Canadian friends, who had waited there for a day in order that they might travel with us. They had breakfast ready for us in a missionary guest-house. Dr Murray and Mother went shopping and sight-seeing, while I was taken charge of by Dr Outerbridge of the theological college and hurried off, first in a taxi to see a little of the town and two of the large Japanese churches, then at top speed up an escalator (I nearly missed the top step once, and forgot to walk once, thinking that it ought to do all the work like an elevator!) through tunnels, along platforms and finally in an electric car and away out to the country, and then in a taxi up hill and brae to see the large United Mission College with thousands of students and a beautiful new college for women students. It was breathless rush and we never stopped for a moment until I was getting exhausted. We set out after eleven o'clock for Shimonoseki and the boat for Korea.

That day in the train by the shores of the inland sea was one of the most memorable throughout this wonderful journey. It was a great thing that we had company. We also had plenty of room. It was like Lough Erne or Killarney all the way. The trees, the crops, the villages, the water, the hills, the light, all were perfect. What joy it was to do the journey by day and to be able to look at the glorious scenery, the most beautiful in Japan, all day long until the sunset in its splendour came and drew the curtain lest our eyes and brains should grow tired of the unending beauty.

We reached the boat. What crowds there were! Fortunately they weren't all going by our vessel, but even so, they swarmed like bees. We had been unable for lack of time to get berths, but were encouraged to hope that some might be available on our arrival; but the stewards smiled when we enquired. Berths indeed! Standing room seemed to be at a premium! We took possession of three cushioned seats which with the corridor formed the frame for a large table and by the time we got our baggage and ourselves deposited there was little room left. The table was covered with little bowls and teapots and there was hot weak tea in the pots. Gradually things got straightened out and most of the Japanese and Koreans settled down on mats and pillows. We on our cushioned benches were not nearly as comfortable. After a good while Mother and I got chairs and pillows in the saloon and we slept for several hours.

There was a strong breeze but not enough to make anybody sick and we had quite a good crossing to Busan which we reached early in the morning on Sunday. As we did not want to travel on Sunday we stayed at the Australian Presbyterian mission house for the day. After breakfast we drove out several miles to a mission station where there is a vocational school for girls. They keep goats, pigs, poultry and rabbits. They look after them themselves and do all the farm work. The Korean girl who accompanied us was in the U.S.A. for some years. In the afternoon we drove several miles and then walked through the rice fields to a Leper Settlement, where there are six hundred lepers looked after by Dr McKenzie, a Scot connected with the Australian Mission. He was at college with Donald Frazer and Wylie Blue. We were at the service which was attended by some hundreds of lepers. I said a few words which Mr McKenzie translated. After a full day we took the night train to Seoul which we reached on Monday morning. And there we must stop.

Thanks, again and again for the lovely letters. The lost one has turned up alright. Glad you all had good holidays. Hope you will have a good term at school and Jack at Trinity. Love from Daddy

Korea and Manchuria

When RHB and AHB left Japan at the end of September they continued to travel through the Japanese Empire. Korea, then one country, had been a Japanese colony since 1910. They were able to travel to Pyongyang, then the centre of Christianity in Korea, but today the capital of North Korea.

RHB and AHB then travelled to Manchuria where they spent six weeks. In 1936 Manchuria was known as Manchukuo and had become a puppet state of Japan. The governor-general mentioned in the next letter must have been Japanese. RHB first wrote about Manchuria in 1909, before he had visited the country. In 1940 RHB published a story of the Irish mission called Waymakers in Manchuria. *In*

1947 in Through Gates of Hope *he describes how the church in Manchuria suffered during the Second World War.*

6

The Presbyterian Church in Ireland Mission
Kirin
Manchuria
October 1st 1936

Dear Robin,

My last letter left us at Busan where we spent Sunday.

In the evening we resumed our journey and travelled during the night to Seoul. I had written beforehand to Dr Clarke of the Christian Literature Society, with whom we were to stay, telling him when we would arrive, but he did not get my letter in time to meet the train. It did not matter, for there were lots of Canadian and American missionaries on the platform and they looked after us.

There were meetings of what is called the Federal Council being held in Seoul and there were people from all over Korea there. We were sent to the house of Dr and Mrs Boots and we stayed with them while we were in Seoul. Dr Boots is a dentist and is the missionary at the head of the dental school or college, connected with the Severance Hospital, one of the great Medical Missions and Colleges. We saw the hospital. It is a very big institution with hundreds of patients every day and a large number of American and Korean doctors and nurses on the staff. We went to the meetings and met many people. The Vice Governor-General visited the Council and gave an address, and the Governor–General gave a tea party to which we were invited and went. We stayed two days in Seoul and saw a great many things. We liked the old Korean Gate in the centre of the town and an old pagoda in a garden which was shown to us at night. The dress of the Koreans was fascinating – long flowing robes as white as snow.

From Seoul we went to Pyengyang and were met at the station by Mr Hamilton of the American Presbyterian Mission. On the way to his house he brought us round by the river and up a cork-screw hill to show us one of the loveliest sights in the world. The speed at which we were driven round the corners was dazzling. When we got to the top of the hill we wondered when we would see the marvellous view. He said, 'It's there, but the bargain with the taxi driver was that we should not stop!' I suppose we can see the view at greater leisure next time.

In Pyengyang we went to a street-chapel and saw how it was carried on. At night we saw a prayer-meeting in one of the churches with over 500 present, and at 4.30 in the morning we heard the church bells calling people to church. We did not go! Then we saw schools and colleges and hospitals and met all the missionaries of the station and some of their children at a weekly meeting which I had to address. Next morning we started early leaving at 7.20. We journeyed on all day and at 4.20 in the afternoon we reached Moukden. It was most delightful journey. There were green hills, flowing streams, and fields of rice and millet ripe with the harvest. The colours were beautiful, but Mother can tell you more about them than I can.

… We were met at Moukden station by Mr and Mrs Miskelly, Mr Stevenson and Mr Fulton. They gave us a great welcome. After a while they got us into a small carriage "drosky" drawn by a small pony and brought us to Mr Stevenson's house where we felt at home.

We remained there till the Monday afternoon. It was supposed to be a resting time and we did not do much but write letters and READ those that were waiting for us! They gave us all the news up to 9th of September. I thought we had got all you had written, but another letter sent from Milford reached us here today, so that now we have them all.

On Sunday morning we went to church. The pastor preached but we did not know what he was saying. Some of the tunes were familiar: "All hail the power of Jesus Name". "Crown Him with many crowns". I suppose the words were much the same as the English. The text was His Name shall be called wonderful. A Scottish lady missionary played the organ. The collection was taken up by men on the men's side and women on the women's side. There are paintings of the four seasons on the windows done by Mrs Inglis. The communion table is the gift of Dr Fleming Fulton of Knock.

At five o'clock there was an English service in the Scottish Medical College for all the missionaries. I took the service. It was a great pleasure to meet so many people whose names I have known for a long time.

On Monday I went with Mr Miskilly to the Manchuria Christian College. A new section with classrooms on the first floor and an assembly hall on the second had just been built. The students met in the hall and there was a good turnout of them at eight o'clock. I was introduced to them but had only to bow, as I am to pay a second visit later.

Most of Monday morning was spent in preparation for our next move. At 1.50 we left Moukden for Kirin in the great Express, the Asia, one of the best trains in the world. Mr Stevenson booked our seats early. In four hours we had only one stop at Hsinking, the capital. There we changed into another train which left for Kirin at six o'clock, and we arrived at nine. We were met at the station by Mr McWhirter, the Sloans and Mr Blakely. Since we came to Kirin we have been out seeing things every morning; but it would take another letter to tell you all about that and this one had better go off soon. Jack will be away in Dublin. Send the letter to him and he can return it to you when he has read it.

Many thanks for the letters we have got and for the illustrations. We are looking forward to the next post and hope it will bring good news and plenty of it.

Our dearest love to you all,
Dads

7

Kirin, Manchuria
October 2nd 1936

Dear Honor,

I have written the long letter to Robin. I hope you will be able to read it. We have been very busy today and had a Chinese feast in a restaurant, about thirty persons present. It was a very long affair with about fifteen courses, including sea slugs, lotus seeds, bamboo shoots, pork, fish, shrimps, rice and I know not what else. It lasted for a long time and was interesting. Yesterday was a lovely day and we went down to the river to a hill for tea. The country looked beautiful and the sun was bright and warm. Today it was much cooler, with dust and wind. Before the feast was over it was raining and it has poured ever since. You could not imagine what the roads are like! We are just going out to Mr Blakely's for dinner. Early tomorrow morning we will leave here for Hsinking, the capital, and we will stay there until Wednesday.

With much love to you all,
Daddy

PTO Honor. The Carthage will sail from Shanghai on Nov 24th. You ought to call at the C.P.R. office in Donegall Place and ask them to tell you the last date for posting letters to catch the Carthage at Shanghai, Singapore, Colombo, Bombay, and send a letter to each place. If you tell them who you are they will take a lot of trouble to get you the information exactly. I'll send them a note about it. Dads

8

Newchwang
Manchuria
11/10/36

My dear Honor,

So much has happened since I wrote nearly a week ago that I scarcely remember where I left off, and hardly know where I am! I think, however, that we had left Kirin on a bitterly cold morning and had been met at Hsinking and welcomed there by Mr Johnston, Harold Corkey and some members of the church.

We had a very busy time at Hsinking. My first duty was to preach at the harvest thanksgiving service in the Gillespie Memorial Church, which was built a few years ago in memory of Mr Gillespie, an uncle of the girl who was head girl at Victoria. There was a lot of fruit and vegetables which was either sold for the church or given to the poor of the congregation. The church was well filled with people. There was a choir, also a man with a trumpet, who kept the singing up to time, but rather disturbed the organist by blowing so close to her ear. All sorts of classes of young people sang their special hymns. It was a great sight.

In the afternoon I had to preach again in a small mission church away in another district. I baptised Caroline Louise Corkey, a lovely baby, who was perfect in her behaviour. It took a long time to see the day schools, the Bible schools, the Women's Hospital and so on. We need a new men's hospital and a new doctor soon. Hsinking is now the capital of Manchukuo. There are dozens of new roads being made and thousands of buildings large and small being put up. Some of the buildings are immense and no money is being spared by the Japanese to make the city one of the largest and grandest.

Before leaving Hsinking I sent off a cablegram for the Rally on Thursday last. "Best wishes for a successful rally: Cannot too strongly urge the necessity of strengthening medical work. Boyds". I hope it reached home in time. I left a clear margin of two days. One of our most delightful meetings was a tea party attended by many preachers, teachers, Bible-women, missionaries and members of the congregations. It was to welcome us and the Corkeys who have only recently arrived. In replying I did not speak

RHB and AHB on their wedding day in Surat, 7 January 1915.

RHB and AHB with wedding guests.

RHB, AHB and Jack, 1919

The S.S. Naldera, one of the ships RHB and AHB sailed in during their 1936–1937 voyage round the world.

The Boyd family at Ballycastle, 1938. Standing: Jack, Billy, Robin. Seated: RHB, Honor, AHB.

RHB in Moderator's robes and garlanded, with visiting Indian Presbyterian Delegation, Church House, Belfast 1947.

The Moderator visits Boys' Auxiliary camp, Castlerock, 1947.

RHB baptized his first grandson, John Robert Boyd Hanna, Belfast, 1954.

Standing: Rev Robin Boyd, Rev William Hanna, Rev William Boyd, RHB. Seated: Frances Boyd, Honor Hanna (with John), AHB.

RHB and AHB out for a country walk, Northern Ireland, 1957.

RHB at Church House on his last day as Convener of the Foreign Mission.

Manuscript of "While I Remember" in which
RHB describes first meeting with Gandhi.

Author with his grandfather, Northern Ireland, summer 1957.

Windsor Presbyterian Church and Manse, Belfast. The Manse is now owned by the Peace People.

Gujarat

*Author in Surat 2012, searching for where
the wedding photos of RHB and AHB were taken.*

*Were these the steps where the wedding photo
of RHB and AHB was taken in 1915?*

The bungalow at the Irish Presbyterian Mission, Ahmedabad, where Mary Honor Boyd was born in 1921.

Visiting the primary school founded by IP missionaries, Anand 2012.

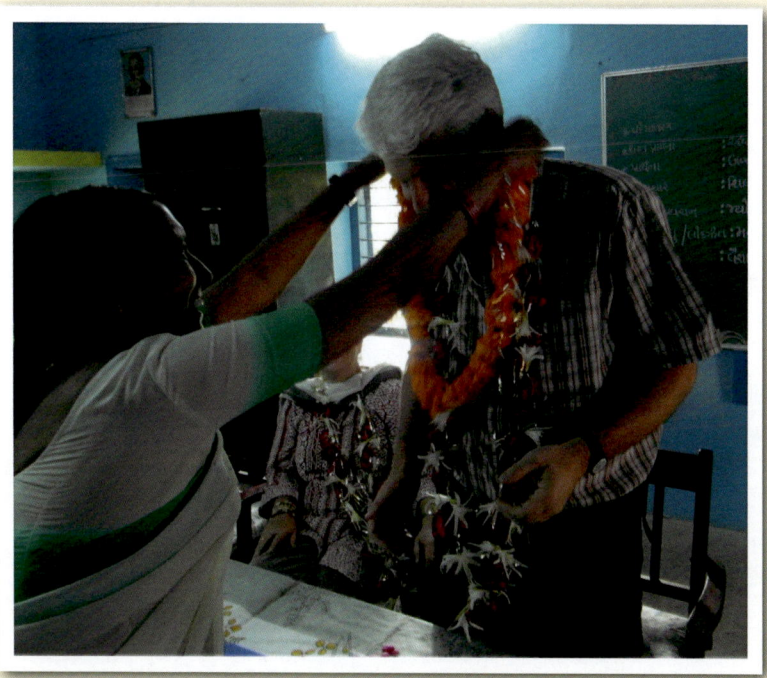

"Fooled again" in Borsad, 2012.

Myanmar/Burma

Captain Jack Boyd, 13th Frontier Force Regiment, India 1941.

Taukkyan Commonwealth War Graves Cemetery, outside Rangoon, Myanmar/Burma.

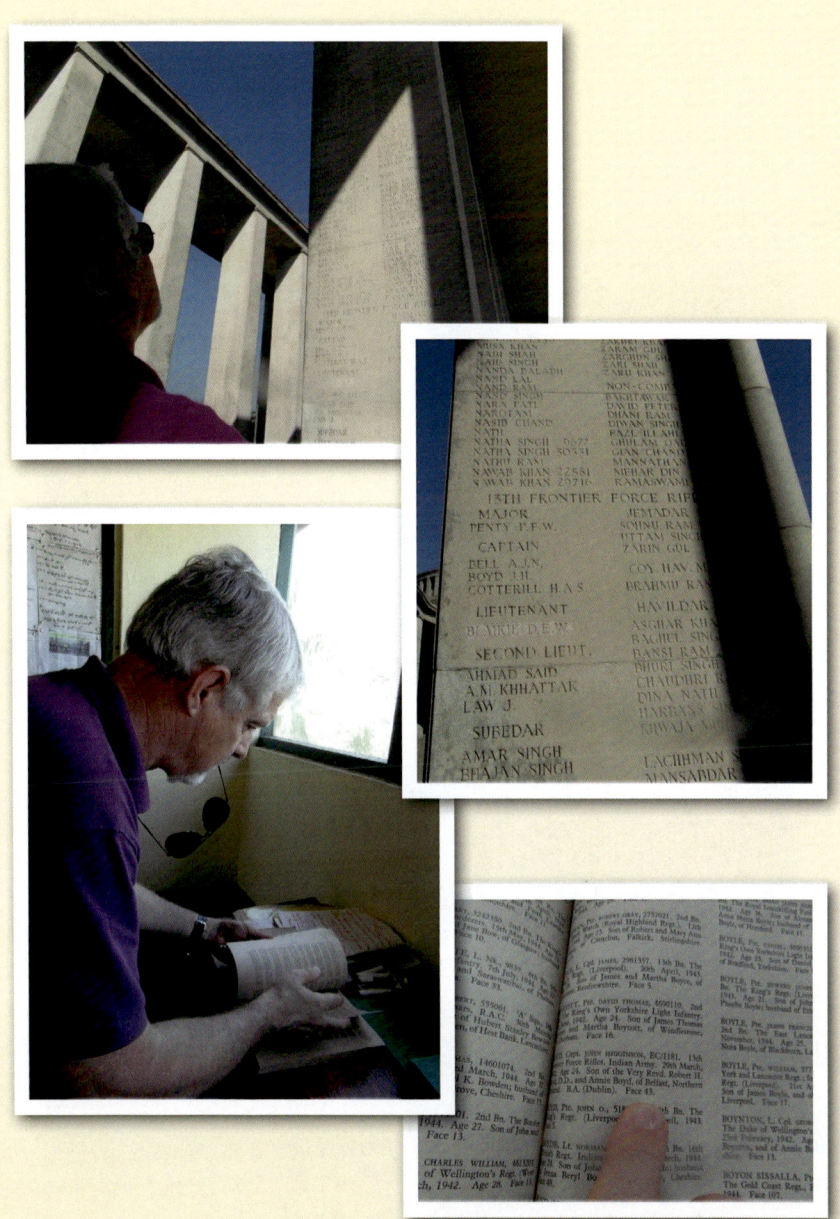

Finding Jack Boyd's name in Burma.

Laying flowers on the grave of a soldier "Known unto God".

sentence by sentence but said all I had to say in one go and then let Mr Johnston give the substance of it. I said that I could not wait for my speech to trickle out slowly like drops from a stopped tap. I wanted them to rush out in one great spate! Mr Johnston tried to translate that and ended up by saying: 'If you want to know what Dr Boyd's feelings are, just look at his face!' Mother also spoke. It was a delightful evening.

We left Hsinking by the "Asia". When we started we had not the stream-lined engine, but it was attached at Moukden. It is a great train, doing an average of fifty miles per hour, but much more than that on certain parts of the line. There were tourist Bureau booklets in the corridor and I gathered up a few to send home to Robin and Billy. Half an hour in another train brought up to Yinkow. We all got into a taxi, the driver of which was wakened from his slumbers with difficulty and we travelled safely to Mr McCammon's house.

It was a tremendous joy to get all the letters here. We got two batches of them at the same time, so we had a great feast. I was glad to know that Mittens had been seen and I hope he will get some sense and return to his own home. Rab will be comfortable, I hope, during the winter. He will not get so wet on a rainy day. The mosquitos will like Caesar's army have gone into winter quarters by this time. The long grass must have harboured them. Jack should get the lawn-mower sharpened and set. It is too late now for this year. Congratulations for your promotion in Guides and best wishes for your success. You have our hearts' love all the time. Two months are now over, and time is flying very fast because we are so busy. In another month we will

be leaving Manchuria. Share this letter with Jack and try to keep all the letters together.
   Dearest love
   Daddy

9

Fakumen
19/10/36

Dear Honor,
   We got the letters in Moukden while we were there and they filled our cup to overflowing. The news was good, but I hope you will stop taking things! What all have you had? Several of the plagues of Egypt, it seems to me. We sympathise with Dr Sara and Miss Margaret. Tell them I hope they will be able to last out until March! Good for Eleanor Megaw; give her my congratulations; I hope Margaret is well. She would undoubtedly have purchased some of the things the medicine man was selling today: snakes, tortoises and dried frogs. I am sorry I can't give his prescriptions, so that she might turn medicine vendor.
   There was another feast in our honour last Wednesday. I could not begin to tell you about the fifteen to twenty courses. There were no sea slugs this time. We began, of course, with buried eggs. There were several courses of fish, fried and boiled and a very slithery course made from fishes' lips. There was chicken in several forms and other such dainties as preserved dates, meat dumplings, sugar cane shoots, asparagus, lotus seeds ending with a whole chicken in soup and a bowl of rice. At these feasts the rice comes last, and although there has been so much before it, yet one is supposed to finish the bowlful and ask for

more! I was able to finish mine this time. I have made such progress that I was able to use chopsticks and was no longer ashamed of myself and my country!

If you have a 1937 Prayer Calendar, which I have not yet seen, you will find all about Fakumen in it and you will see what we have seen. We often wonder about Mrs Crawford. If she is still there, remember us to her. Love to everybody and that includes YOU.

Love again
Daddy

10

Hsin Min
Manchuria
26/10/36

Dear Jack,

Honor will send the long letter to you. We are both very well and enjoying the hospitality of very kind people. We are now fairly familiar with the lie of the land, but the lack of language is a great barrier. There have been many schools to see and many groups to meet. We are just going out to one now.

… We are almost gasping for letters from home to tell us how you all are. I hope you are having a very happy and useful session in Trinity. Make the most of it, get all you can, for college days do not return. We hope to hear all about your plans and whether you changed your rooms or not.

Remember me to friends in Dublin, the Rutherfords if you see them and the Breakeys, the McNabs and the Lyles.

Much love from us both
Your loving Father

11

Dear Honor
> EXTRA SPECIAL EDITION

It is Monday morning the 26th of October. One of the first thoughts that came into my mind this morning was: a month from today we will be on our way to Bombay.

Yesterday afternoon the headmistress invited us to a meeting of the senior girls. There were speeches and hymns and we had to say 'Thank you very much for your welcome'. Mother spoke first and said 'Thank you' very nicely. It was a girls' meeting and her speech ought to have been enough, but they demanded one from me too. So I said: 'When a man's wife has spoken there is not much left for him to say except I agree entirely with the previous speaker,' which I do. Then I told them one of the reasons I was so glad to see them was because they were all wearing blue. 'At home we have a daughter who goes to school. The colour of her school's uniform is blue, and so when we look at you we just think that each one of you is our own daughter.' That got me started and I told them about Captain Cook and how he made gardens and had one day the pleasure of eating potatoes and turnips for dinner in a South Sea Island. Our missionaries had come to Manchuria and had planted gardens in which they had sown the good seed of the Word. It was our great joy to see the flowers growing up, and we hoped the pupils would also plant gardens wherever they might go. All of which you have heard before!

Well, dear Eyebright, we never forget you. May Richmond Lodge prosper and may you help it! Love to Emily, Selina and all the others.

Ever your loving,
Dads

12

Chinksien
Manchuria
Nov 3rd 1936

Dear Honor

I am sitting in a low chair with arms and Mother is at the table. Our room has two good windows facing the south and a large alcove with a window that can open into the garden on the east. There is central heating and there is also a fire! I hear an aeroplane, probably the daily one that flies from Moukden to Shanhaikuan and makes a stop here. The garden is now bare and empty but it must have been lovely when all the flowers were out a month ago and the lovely vines and creepers still had all their leaves on. There were thousands of nasturtiums and other colourful flowers. Now they are all over except a few cosmos that withstood the first assault of frost. All the green vegetables have been raised and put into a large cellar or pit dug in the ground, covered with sticks and millet stalks and banked up with soil. There is a door left for a man to enter and get out with the cabbage and carrots when they are needed during the winter. In a few weeks snow will be here and winter will remain until April. Double windows, sealed ventilators and the like will keep Jack Frost out. We have escaped him up till now, but he may get us yet.

Love to you all and may you have great happiness at school. I hope the work is not too hard.

Ever your loving,

Father

13

Moukden
Manchuria
9/11/36

Dear Jack and all of you,

We are now in Moukden. This is the last of our stations and in two days we shall leave for China on our way to India. When we arrived there we had some delay in getting out and Dr Fulton and others who had come to meet us were delayed in getting in. On the platform a number of men in uniform were drawn up in order, waiting for the arrival of some important person – not us! Important looking people, some of them in uniform and others wearing silk hats and appropriate clothes got out of the train and saluted those on the platform and were saluted by them. Then a procession was formed and all the important persons walked reverently behind someone carrying an object with great care and reverence. It was a portrait of the Emperor of Manchukuo, which was being brought to Chinksein to be put up in some public office or school. A number of them arrived the previous evening and had been suitably received. About the same time some hundred of them have been sent out to different places. They are hung up in schools and covered with yellow cloth and on certain occasions they are saluted. It was interesting to see the great respect with which the portrait is treated.

Returning Dr Fulton stopped at a fruit shop to purchase some persimmons. He had noted our fondness for them "at breakfast, dinner and tea". We were greatly interested in the way he purchased them. The shopkeeper showed him some that looked over ripe. He said he would not take them. The shopkeeper said they were perfect for Chinese use. Dr Fulton said that if we foreigners should eat them like that there would be a war inside of us. The shopkeeper laughed and said he did not come to the country yesterday! Dr Fulton then took up each one separately and felt it all over, looked at it and weighed it in his hand and put it on one side. Then they had to be paid for and that also took time and jokes and smiles. As we came away the shopkeeper and his staff came outside the door of the shop and bowed. We also bowed, and except for the absence of afternoon tea, it looked as if we had been paying a call. Quite likely tea was offered, for that is done on every possible occasion. It is quite polite to take it in both hands and set it down untasted.

The time had now come for our departure from Chinsein but we decided to stay a day longer in order to visit a suburb where Mission work is in its early stages and where there is no church. We visited a number of Christian families. In one of them some of the neighbours were invited in to hear. A Biblewoman prayed. At the close of her prayer another woman said: "What was she doing, to whom was she talking?" The Biblewoman was glad to be able to tell her and I am sure she will meet her again and tell her more. That was one of the most touching things I have experienced.

We visited two other homes. Up till then we had successfully overcome the tendency of the householders to make tea, but at last we were beaten. When we reached the last house but one, a very tidy house, with a very dapper little husband retired from business, and a strong capable-looking wife, the cups were on the table and the tea in the flask. I was quite glad to get a drink of this coloured hot water, although I had been doing nothing but listening to other people talking in Chinese. That can be very tiresome. The lady of the house and her husband came out with us and accompanied or followed us until they had to be told to go home, and it took a good deal of telling. The next family have a shop. The younger son unfortunately is addicted to drugs. He had toothache and took the wretched thing to cure it or to ease the pain. Thus he got the habit. He looked as if he had partly overcome it but one never knows. Some forms of it are seldom cured.

On Wednesday morning we packed and finished our letters and at 11.50 we got the "Empress" for Moukden. Representatives of the church, hospital and schools came to the station to see us off, and some of the children were standing in a row outside the station to wave us farewell. Dr Fulton was there and we could not prevent him from doing the work of the porters. He is a marvel at eighty-one, and fifty-three years in Manchuria. The Empress was comfortable. We had a meal in the dining saloon and sat there most of the way looking out through the large clear windows. In a few hours we were in Moukden. Here we have been since, busy, so busy that we will be glad to get away!

We are both well and send our love,
Dads

14

Moukden
Manchuria
11/11/36

Dear Honor,

I am sending the long letter to Jack. I hope it will reach you safely and soon. We are busy packing up just as we did when leaving home. Tonight we bid goodbye to Manchukuo and go to Peking for a few days. Then on to Shanghai and Bombay. We are wondering if your precious letters will come here this week and we are dreading the possibility of their not reaching us before we go.

Our programme has been s t r e n u o u s. I ought to have written it in capitals and just three heavy lines under it! We have kept very well, and we have done all that we were asked to do. So I suppose we are still unprofitable servants! I hope to get time in Shanghai to bring my letter up to date, although I am afraid the days are blank in the diary.

We send our dearest love to you all. Remember us to all friends.

Your loving Father

China, Singapore and Malaya

After Manchuria RHB and AHB spent a week in Peking, where they saw the Great Wall and the Altar of Heaven, but found no letters awaiting them. They had "great good luck" with two sets of letters arriving in Shanghai. In reply RHB had advice for Honor:

> When this Junior is over you will have a better idea of what you can do. No matter what you do you will have lots of work before you are through with it. In the meantime, get as much strength as you can; keep in the open air when possible, and walk, w a l k, W A L K. While doing that it will do you no harm to spell, spell, spell.

In Shanghai they stayed in a private hotel called Beumans which had "seen better days, but was all right" and they got lost walking and seeking for directions, so that they were almost late for church.

From Shanghai they travelled to Hong Kong, on board the S.S. Naldera, from where they sent Jack a letter-card with pictures of the Second Class Dining Saloon, the Second Saloon Music Room, Second Smoking room and Second Promenade deck. RHB was amused that his cabin was number forty-one, like the number of his house in Osborne Park, Belfast. Miss Rogers appears as a companion for AHB.

15

S.S. *Naldera*
29th November 1936

Dear Boyd Family,

We sent off our last letter at Hong Kong, via Siberia, and, in order that this may not be too long an interval we hope to send this one by air mail from Singapore. That will shorten the time considerably. If we posted in the ordinary way you would not get it till after the 26th of December, as it would go all the way to Marseilles by this boat. We have had a very quiet voyage till the present. The weather has been delightful. Today there is a little bit of a swell, but the sea is blue with lovely white crests on the waves and white foam near the ship. There are great white clouds in the sky that soften the heat and glare of the sun, and there is also a very pleasant breeze. Never before, I think, have we travelled with so few passengers, and as everybody seems to be engaged about his own business there is not much going on.

In Hong Kong we stayed at the Hong Kong Hotel which has a beautiful situation overlooking the bay. We had lunch in the hotel and then sat in the garden for a while. After a while we went down to the shore. Mother and Miss Rogers took off their shoes and stockings and paddled. Later Mother and I went to the Lido and got bathing suits and towels and bathed. The water was not warm, but it was not nearly as cold as we are accustomed to. Afterwards I glowed all over instead of shivering as I would have done last July at Portballintrae. On the way back in a tram I spoke to two young soldiers of the Royal Ulster Rifles. One of them comes from the Shankhill Road and the other was "rared" in the Free State, across from Fermanagh.

On Friday morning we did not cross over to Hong Kong but spent the morning on the Kowloon side visiting the shops and asking the prices of things, especially of small blue ducks! It took a long time to see them all, but that is not my part of the story. We also looked at some carved camphor-wood chests, but neither does that come into my province.

I got tired at half past ten and returned to the *Naldera* to look at the small boats, chiefly in charge of women and children that swarmed round the *Naldera* begging for money and apples and gathering up all the scraps of food that were thrown into the sea. At the same time coal was being put in. It must be a wonderful life that people have on the little boats. The whole family is there and even very small children are able to beg. In one boat a boy was performing as an acrobat. On another was a bigger boy who dived for coins and generally got them. Some of the boats had a lot of birds in cages for sale. An oldish sort of man, who appeared to me to be blind or nearly so, kept a cage balanced on his hand and for a long time sat as if he was listening and staring. The Chinese are fond of doing that, and it is not a bad thing just being able to sit and stare! That is one of the characteristics of the Chinese that I almost possess. As I stood and stared the time passed and twelve o'clock came. Mother and Miss Rogers and, I believe, a flock of green ducks, came on board.

Another day has passed. The sea is calm, but there is a kind of stickiness that reminds me of the monsoon in India. It will continue till we get away from Pennay. We are now settled down to the routine of the ship. The cabin boy comes at 7.30 with orange juice. After that I get up, shave, bathe and dress. There is no tram to catch, no appointment to keep and no need for hurry.

Up till now our thoughts have been about Manchuria. Now they are turning to Gujarat. Tomorrow at 10.30 we are due in Singapore. When we reach Singapore we expect to get a letter from Aunt Ena and Uncle Andrew telling us the best way to travel. We ought to have the whole of Thursday and Friday with them.

Love to all of you. I hope the Shanghai letters and cards with all their stamps reached you safely. Remember me to Aunt Margaret, Aunt Amy and Aunt Nora, John, Selina and every other body. The best of good wishes to the dog and to the cat when you see him afar off.

Your loving Dads

16

S.S. *Naldera*
Monday Dec 6th 1936

Dear Young People,

It is Monday morning and it is warm. There is bright sunshine and there are clouds. Yesterday we had some rain which made little difference to the heat and added to the moisture, which is very unpleasant and adds to the difficulty of writing. We duly arrived in Singapore on Wednesday morning. An aeroplane circled around us and came quite close. The harbour is beautiful and there is a large amount of shipping in it. We were glad to get some letters from home and very sorry to learn about Professor Haire's illness, although the information we received was very scrappy – namely "Everybody will have already told you, so there is no need for me to do more than merely mention it". Nobody told us and nobody did more than mention it!

We were at first disappointed at not getting a letter from Aunt Ena giving us directions about the train to take for Batu Gajah. Just in time a letter arrived, not through the post, but by the hand of a messenger from the Fiat Motor Works in Singapore. The letter told us that Uncle Andrew's car was out of action for a couple of days, but he had asked the Fiat manager in Singapore to make arrangements for a car and driver to bring us up as soon as we were ready to start. We were supplied with a "Terraplane", a driver, and a man to accompany him and we decided to start from Raffles Hotel after lunch. We got off about 1.30 on the longest drive we have ever done at once. The road is excellent and the scenery is just what you would expect: palm trees of various kinds, rubber plantation, banana trees, and jungle. Water, water everywhere, and in among the trees the Malayans' houses, thatched with palm leaves and raised up from the ground and above the water on props like stilts.

> *The two-day 400-mile round trip was dangerous and full of incidents.*

Twice we almost ran into level-crossing gates, and once we had a heart-thumping experience as we turned a corner at something like forty and suddenly came upon a narrow bridge over a stream. We escaped the near side of the bridge and pulled up just in the nick of time to save ourselves from striking the off-side. We did not know any Chinese and the driver knew only a word or two of English, so our breath was wasted. Mother was tremendously brave over it all.

> *RHB and AHB spent an uncomfortable night in a sticky, cheap hotel room, trying to avoid mosquitos, but eventually made it safely to the comfort of Riverside Estate where RHB's sister, Ena, and brother-in-law, Andrew, welcomed them.*

I would not attempt to tell you of all the kindness which was shown to us during our stay. We were sent to our room and then tea was sent after us. Our room has a mosquito-proof apartment inside, so that it is possible to sleep in comfort without curtains. After a rest and a bath we went down for tea on the lawn and then looked around the garden at the beautiful flowering shrubs. In the evening we sat on the verandah, also mosquito proof and talked and listened to music and news from London on the wireless.

RHB gave an account of the work of the rubber estates, going into great detail on how the "coolies" collect the latex and then transform it into rubber. He also described a Chinese tin mine.

On Friday evening Ryder Boyd, who is the district officer at Batu Gajah came for dinner and it was a pleasure to meet him. We passed through Kuala Lampur where his brother, Rob, is. Had we known we could have called, short as our time was, but we had no idea of his location. On Saturday morning we set out for Penang. Uncle Andrew drove. Aunt Ena came too. Uncle Andrew's car is a Standard 16. It was quite up to standard and brought us in great comfort to Penang – 130 miles. Once we left Ipoh we went straight on through lovely scenery to Taiping where they get 200 inches of rain in a year. We got some of it, also lunch in the rest house. We went for a drive round Penang, a lovely place, and ended with tea in the Runnymede Hotel, with a terrace like the promenade at Newcastle. The sea was fully in when we were there and the breeze as delicious as the tea. We went back to the *Naldera*, bade goodbye about 6.30 to our very good friends. We sailed at seven, and have been going on with very close weather ever since. A notice has just been put up before me while I write: *Naldera* is expected to arrive at Colombo at 6.30 a.m. Wednesday.

Tuesday 7/12/36

Last night was by far the warmest and most oppressive we have yet had in all our travels. It was really warm and even with two electric fans buzzing and blowing it was almost impossible to sleep. Mother went up on deck to get a breeze, but there was nothing there. The wind was following us and we were just going fast enough to keep out of its reach! That is what it felt like. Rain fell early in the morning and it was a bit cooler from six o'clock. I hope the cool winds will travel a bit more quickly today.

We were delighted to get the home letter and one from Aunt Charlotte at Penang. We were very sorry to learn about Aunt Amy's accident. It must have been a great shock to her and Aunt Nora too. Give her my love and best wishes for a quick and complete recovery.

After all the travelling we have done it is difficult to realise that in a few weeks we shall be in Bombay and hard at work on the programme. I'll stop now and resume this volume after Colombo. It will catch the airmail at Bombay and will bring our news up to date.

Love to all of you,
Dads

When I transcribed these letters in 2019, and sent them to the Boyd family, I quizzed Uncle Billy about my own memories of Uncle Andrew, and about some of the items AHB purchased in 1936. I have inherited the camphor chest, but what about the family of ducks? Here is his reply:

Dear Willie,

Two ducks sit solemnly on our bathroom windowsill, one large and one small. The middle-sized duck had an accident many years ago, indeed RHB may have been to blame or one of his offspring. It was never talked about. We think they came to us via Aunt Kathleen, Mother's youngest sister. AHB must have given them to her at some point and we helped clear her house in Wicklow.

According to my faulty memory, Andrew Buchanan, a Scottish rubber planter in Malaya, joined up and was badly wounded in WW1. He was attracted to one of his nurses called Ena Boyd who then had to look after him for the rest of her life. They settled in Malaya. He was in the Reserves and was immediately called up with the rank of captain when Japan came into the war. Stationed in Singapore he was captured and taken prisoner to work on the Burma Railway. Ena came back to Ireland and served as a nurse in a rehab centre for wounded soldiers in Co. Tyrone. Andrew had a rough time, though, he got out of physical labour and did clerical work but suffered a lot of abuse. He was desperately thin and ill when repatriated at the end of the war against Japan. They stayed with us in No.41 and then they rented a little house in Donaghadee and Ena got him back to good health. While in captivity he planned his dream house, every detail, with all manner of tropical timbers and the most modern facilities. But reality struck. Tight building regulations in 1945 forbade anything but the most modest of homes. However, he was his own clerk of works and very determined and he built a lovely little house, about 900 square feet and he acquired one piece of polished oak about six feet long for a window ledge of which he was immensely proud.

His site is right on the water's edge. The house, which has since been completely rebuilt, had a glorious sea view. Ena was a very small person and the house was quite tiny and they lived very simply. He would walk to the village and the Golf Club. There was not much display of wealth. Plastic was beginning to replace rubber, commodity prices were volatile, as were share prices and I am a bit sceptical about his alleged fortune. 'If you are not in the market, get out of it,' he told me, and he bought annuities. They lived happily but Ena got a bad cancer and died shortly before RHB. Andrew had a housekeeper coming in every day and when he died she made sure Honor and I could choose a memento or two. Ena had made sure that Honor, Robin and I would get £1000 each for our children. Libby and Clare decreed that each one of the nine grandchildren should get £333 6s 8d, and so it was. Eventually Andrew became confused and went into the mental hospital in Downpatrick, where he died. We were very fond of them both.

Return to India

17

Bradhwan Camp
Kathiawar
India
18/12/36

Dear Jack, Honor, Robin & Billy,

    I am afraid I am not able to give you all the details of the past week. So much has happened and there was so little time for writing that my letter got behind and now there is no time to overtake it. We reached Bombay at eight o'clock on Friday evening. Up till then the voyage was as pleasant as possible.

    The cabin was a bit hot for a couple of days and nights, but as we neared Bombay there was coolness in the air. We had a busy time packing and getting everything in order, on Friday. Dinner was earlier than usual so that we might be free as soon as the boat arrived. I went along to wait for the arrival of the pilot. I asked some of the Laskars in Gujarati when he would come on board. They replied in Gujarati and I found that forty of them came from Gogha. They knew Mr Beatty and were greatly interested when I told them that his daughter and her husband had joined the ship at Colombo on their way home from their honeymoon in Ceylon.

The pilot arrived and it was not long till we were being brought alongside the pier at Bombay. It took a good while to get our ship safely berthed and as we drew nearer we could see some people, behind iron bars, waiting. After a while we picked out one particular group as ours and by degrees we recognised Mr Brolly, Mr and Mrs Lyle, John Davey and Elizabeth, and some Indians who had come to welcome us. Mr and Mrs Rogers were there too. As soon as our passport was attended to and the gangway was ready for traffic we met and it was a very hearty meeting as you can imagine.

It had been suggested that we might go as far as Broach the first night and then on to Parantij on Monday, but it was decided in the end that we go on to Parantij at once. We got our baggage through the customs in good time to catch the train at the Central Station, but there was such a large number of people travelling that we had difficulty in getting sleeping accommodation.

In the end we did get an upper and lower berth in a compartment with only one fellow traveller. The Daveys had brought pillows and sheets and towels for us, and with our rugs under us or over us we were as comfortable as possible and we slept some. Early in the morning we woke up to see Anand station, and about six o'clock we were in Ahmedabad. We went to the refreshment room and got some tea and toast and soon we were ready for the last part of the journey.

It is forty-one miles by train from Ahmedabad to Parantij, but the train does not hurry, as although we left Ahmedabad at 7.40, we did not reach Parantij till 10.14. That, as we learned later, was really fast for the Ahmedabad-Parantij railway-metre-gauge. The journey was very pleasant and seemed short. We were busy all the time looking and listening and before we reached our destination many faded memories had been revived. The trees were the same as ever and the animals – cows, buffaloes, camels, sheep, goats, monkeys. The birds also were familiar, the doves and pigeons, minas, king-crows etc. So was the noise at the railway stations, and also the language of the people. We were at home once more.

When we got out at Parantij I was reminded of Jack and Honor who spent a few days there with us. We saw the very spot where the engine with its flaming furnace frightened Jack the night we arrived, and we saw big long-tailed monkeys like the one that grinned at us in the bath-room. We were warmly welcomed at the station by Mr Hanna, and many bright willing boys carried off our luggage to the bungalow.

Although this distance is not far we went by car in order to go through a front gate and not in by a back door, as there were people waiting to welcome us. The friends who had met us at Bombay garlanded us there, but it had to be done again and it has been done often since!

It took some time to get settled down and we did nothing on Saturday evening but look round the compound, especially at the new school and hostel in memory of the Rev Dr J.F. Steele which was to be opened in a day or two. I was asked to take one of the services on Sunday, and decided to take the morning one so that I might not have to spend the whole of Sunday in preparation. It is usually held at eight o'clock, but they made it half an hour later to give me time in the morning to oil my tongue and get some of the rust that had accumulated in fourteen years rubbed off.

My sleep was not very sound and I awoke early. I took the whole service and although I had to pause every now and then to search for a word that was unwilling to come, yet it or some other word did come, and I got through quite well, considering the handicaps. In the afternoon Miss Rogers distributed prizes to the Sunday school and I closed the meeting with prayer. In the evening there was a meeting of the sword-bearers at which I had to give a short address. Before night some of the rust was off and the key was working more smoothly in the lock!

In between the last two meetings, Mr Hanna drove us to the cemetery to see once more the lovely Irish cross which was put up by Mr Stevenson in memory of three hundred children who died at Parantij Orphanage during the famine of 1900. It is a beautiful piece of work, well done by Indian workmen, and very touching are the words in Gujarati for "They shall hunger no more".

On Monday we saw schools and after the strenuous Sunday took things fairly easy, for Tuesday was to be the big day and some preparations had to be made for it. Soon after ten o'clock our own folk and representatives of the

Indian Church began to arrive. Most of the missionaries, both men and women, came from Surat, Broach, Borsad, Anand, Cambay, Ahmedabad, Gogha, Rajkot. Dusa was represented by its Indian pastor. From the jungle tribes mission we had Mr McNeill, Mr Robinson, and Dr and Mrs Hazlett. The meeting was held in the church. Mr McNeill was chairman. We sang "The King of Love" and "The Lord's My Shepherd". Mr McNeill spoke, then on behalf of the W.M.A. Miss Colhoun welcomed Mother who spoke, as she always does, in reply. Then the Moderator of presbytery welcomed both of us and I replied in Gujarati. After that Mr Graham and Mr Cromie welcomed us on behalf of the Mission Councils and I had to talk again in English, which I did by telling them something about Korea and Manchuria. That meeting was over about 1.30.

At two o'clock we went to a large mandap – sort of tent – under one of the big trees. There was a large attendance of schoolboys, parents and visitors, some from the town and some from a distance, all there to take part in the opening of the Steele Memorial. Mr Hanna had worked very hard to have everything ready and we were all proud of him and full of admiration of him for his zeal and untiring industry. Mr Beatty presided. Obedbhai spoke about Dr Steele. He gave a long, detailed and most interesting account of him, lit up by a number of recollections. His address was so full and so good that Mr Wilson who followed him had not much scope and gave just a few points and did it excellently. There were various items by some of the boys. My part was in a sentence or two to dedicate the new building and open it. What I said would in English be something like this:

"This house, built to the glory of God and in memory of the Rev J.F. Steele, I, as a representative of the Presbyterian Church in Ireland, dedicate to God."

"This house, built to the glory of God and for the physical, mental and spiritual development of youth, I dedicate to God."

"This house, built in the establishment and extension of the Church of Christ, I dedicate to the Glory of God."

After that Mr. Hanna and I went out, and with a silver key I opened a silver lock and declared the door of the house to be open. Then we returned and I said: 'May the love of God dwell with all who dwell in this house. May the peace of Jesus Christ abide with all who dwell in this house. May the light of the Holy Spirit give knowledge and wisdom to all who dwell in this house.' After each sentence all present said Amen.

These proceedings were followed by the headmaster's report. Mother then presented prizes to the boys who had won them, and shawls of various kinds to the head mason, head carpenter, head blacksmith, head labourer, a woman and a widow, etc. That was followed by garlands, when we, especially Mr. Hanna and ourselves, were almost buried in flowers. My neck is not nearly long enough for this sort of thing! In an hour or two all the visitors had gone. It was a great day and it was a privilege to have a part in its proceedings.

The time is rushing on and I must stop here. If I started to tell you about the cooing of the doves, the creaking of the walls, the pranks of the monkeys, the grunting of the camels, the barking of the dogs, the yelping of the jackals, the emptiness of the threshing-floors on account of the failure of the rains, and so on and on to the squirrels, the flying foxes, the honeybirds, bee-eaters and so forth, there would be no end to this epistle. We have walked under the shade of neem trees and mango trees, on the little-worn paths through the cotton-fields and over to the wells from which one pair or two pairs of oxen were drawing water to irrigate the little plots of land, and there we have heard once more the sad story of crop failure with which I was so familiar in days long gone. The story is the same, and so far as I can see, out in the country things have changed but little. The drum is still beaten and the bells are rung at sunset to put the gods to sleep, and the old Junjari to whom I spoke in the village a few evenings ago is just the same as his brethren were twenty years ago – the same in his routine of idol-worship, the same in his apology for it, the same in his view of the ignorance of the people and the wisdom of keeping them just where they always were. I would just love to begin all over again among these people and to tell them of Him who redeems man's life. As far as I can see the opportunity for doing that is as great as ever.

Love to you all. I'll begin sooner next time!
Dads

> *As Christmas approached RHB and AHB were again carrying out a strenuous programme of engagements, visiting missionary stations, with their churches, schools and hospitals, travelling on trains and dusty roads, being garlanded, giving sermons, "which you will all be very sorry not to read!" After four months*

on the road, RHB still seems to enjoy the trains, no matter how dense the crowds. He observes the countryside with a knowledgeable eye, and is happy to return to places he remembers from his early days as a missionary. But he is fed up with packing!

19

Rajkot
23rd December 1936

Dear Honor and Everybody,

I have almost lost the thread of my story!

We had a delightful time at Parantij and it was time to pack up for the next move.

This packing! When will it cease? Always the same problems present themselves. How much can I do without? What ought to be at the bottom and what at the top? When all is in, will the thing close or will the springs burst? – lugs, I mean, not springs, would that they were springs. And then when all is closed and the key is turned there is that tie, or tooth-brush, or odd slipper – and all of them cannot be put into my pocket! Well, it was late when my brown leather case, and big black case, and mother's brown case and shoe-case, and hat-case, and black zip bag, and flat basket, and straight handed basket, and the hold-all, green, and the other one for bedding, kindly lent by John and Elisabeth Davey, were all packed and ready for the morning.

We slept and were awake early – tea at five or a little later and out to catch the train at six o'clock. We were told not to be in a hurry as the engine driver had to get his tea at Parantij and would not start punctually. He took lots of time to refresh himself, but at last we got off and had a most delightful cool ride to Ahmedabad station. The governor of Bombay was visiting the city that day and his special carriages were conspicuous. They were all closed so we did not see how a governor's saloon is furnished. The train to Veraingam was not crowded. At Veraingam we really felt that we were in India. The crowd on the platform was enormous. What a number of people travel in this country! They were pushing as they used to push and shouting as they always shouted. Close by our carriage were the large water vessels from which thirsty travellers got a drink. Not far away was the tea-counter from which others got a cup of hot tea. All sorts of hawkers, selling matches and cigarettes, Indian sweetmeats, fruit, newspapers, etc. were busy pushing their wares, and people of every cast of countenance and style of dress either sat in the rain or on the platform, or hurried along as if something was lost.

After a long wait our train came in and soon we were on our way to Kathiawar. The country looked parched and bare for lack of rain. It was a bad year. At the beginning of the cold weather there was a storm and some heavy rain that supplied water for the cattle and will be useful for the winter crops, but which destroyed much of what had survived. Some of the remaining cotton was brown and wilted, but near a well it was green and prosperous looking. The farther we went the more Kathiawar resembled itself and the more the people reminded me of the years gone by. The wide open spaces, unlike the closed in appearance in Gujarat, the bare ground, the stunted bushes, contrasted with the hedged-in fields and spreading trees.

The names of some of the stations evoked old memories and at last the village of Dhudrij with its temple towers came into view. It was really thrilling to be in Wadhwan camp again. I remember well the first day I arrived there twenty-five years ago and was met by Sursingh. It was the first time I had been sent out to occupy a station alone and it was a venture. The school, which was also the church then, is now a hospital ward. The bungalow is the same but greatly improved, and the water is much the same in the compound well, undrinkable and good for little or nothing! We were tired after the long journey and the long day, so we did nothing but take a walk away up into the fields along a raised road leading to an old and no longer used shooting range. It used to be my favourite walk when I wanted to get a breeze. The compound was gaily decorated for us with a big W E L C O M E over the gate, and the hospital staff garlanded us. The next day we inspected the Alexander Kerr Memorial Hospital and that was one of our greatest pleasures. It was full of in-patients and there was a large number of out-patients waiting for treatment. We knew a number of the staff: Dr Bharia, whom I knew when he was a student, George Obedbhai, an Anand boy, Andrew Pitamber and others. There all appear to be greatly interested and they have all done good work. The Boys Brigade will be proud of the operating theatre which they are paying for before 1940. From outside the building does not look much yet, but when the second storey is added it will look well with its long verandah and round columns of stone. Nobody who sees it now could refrain from wishing to see it complete, especially as every corner is occupied even now. While we were there the last boxes containing the X-ray equipment arrived. When it is set up and is in operation the usefulness of this hospital will be much increased…

… It was great delight to be in Rajkot where our first home was and where we were welcomed after our wedding. We stayed in the beautiful guest-house, the same one, I think, that we and Uncle Willie stayed in way back in 1915.

If I had time and space I would like to linger for a while near one of the village threshing floors, or under the trees surrounding some of the wells we saw by the way. The green-watered gardens in the midst of the parched country-side were a sight to look at and remember.

Love to you all. There is no time for a separate letter. Good man Billy, first again. I hope the bikes are all right. Glad to get the results Honor. Peg away.

Love again and again more love from Dads

20

Lunawada
29/12/1936

Dear All of you,

I hope you had a very happy Xmas at Beaumond and that the donkey or donkeys is or are nothing the worse, also, that Robin was home early enough to be present at this first period at Inst. We had a very pleasant Christmas in Cambay with the Daveys, but I am sure that Mother has written so much about that that any words of mine are unnecessary…

We had not much to do on Saturday, but in the afternoon we were brought to the palace to meet the Nawab Saheb, the Queen and the heir, a young baby. The Nawab Saheb is a young man, tall and dark with a boyish laugh. After tea he accompanied us through the grounds and showed us some of the improvements he is making in the lawns. He also showed us his horses and his greyhounds. The first time I went to Cambay many years ago there were many lovely horses. Since motors came in there are not so many and we only saw five or six used by His Highness for riding. The greyhounds are not quite purebred and they are not often used for hunting, but their master hopes to be able to sell some of them later.

On Sunday morning I took the service in Cambay Church. In the afternoon we went to Khadana where a number of the Christians had assembled to welcome us. We had the usual songs and garlands.

From Khadana we drove to Anand. What a road! It was getting dark and at times we hardly knew whether we were on the road or not, and it did not matter much, for sometimes we were better off it. The hedges on each side were so close to us that we had to beware lest the thorns should strike us. 'Mind your Eyes!' 'Oh, awfully sorry for that bump.' 'Now I wonder is this the road?' 'We will be all right once we get into the good road!' These were some of the exclamations from the driver as we rolled along at ten or twelve miles an hour. A few miles of the way were so thickly covered with brushwood that it looked as if we were blazing a new trail in the primeval forest.

At last we emerged out of the jungle at a large village and struck the highway leading in one direction to Anand and in another to Borsad. We got up speed now, as the Lough Swilly railway train might down a hill after panting through a highland cutting. There were not many carts or buses, so we had only to swallow our own dust. It was thrilling to get to the part of the road with which we were familiar at Anand. How often did Spark and I travel from and to Naoli, even to and from Borsad, never drawing rein all the way till we crossed the railway line past the lake and into the Medical Mission compound by the back lane? Although there was not room on his back for four of us together with all the luggage we have to carry, it was a pleasant way for one man to travel, and perhaps a good horse was able to go as far as a man ought to want to go, especially on Sunday.

… We got the train to Godra. It took us through Bhali where Jack and his goat used to be well known, through Dakar where we used to get out to drive by tonga to Careypur. I walked it once and got very sore feet. Another time I rode on a borrowed pony about the size of a donkey and missed the train by a minute or two. We had not long to wait at Godra. The little train for Lunawada was waiting when we arrived. We had time to drink some coffee while we waited, and we started to travel in a leisurely sort of way through the jungle, where the chief industry is timber.

We stopped at a number of stations and, up to time, reached Milawada where Mr Graham and some of his workers were waiting to greet us.

(*Here the handwriting becomes a bit smudged*).

How I wish that old pen of mine were near me! This one did well for a while but now it is in such a hurry to supply me with ink that I cannot write fast enough. It would take Ganpati himself to keep up with it.

It was about 3 p.m. when we reached Lunawada and we had not much to do that day. When the sun began to go down we went out for a walk along the raised bank of the town lake. There is very little water this year, as the monsoon rain failed. In a few months people will be in great distress to get water for their cattle and many animals will be allowed to die. One Rajah has advised his farmers to preserve two oxen for work and one buffalo for milk and let the rest starve. They will not kill and they hate selling to the Mohammedan butchers for a rupee or two. In some of the ponds there is so little water that a great part of the space that ought to be filled with it is cultivated so that some green fodder, no matter how little, may be raised…

A Monster Pounces

21

Dohad
8th January 1937

My dear Honor,

The last writing I did was in Garbada, just a week ago. It was too late for the ordinary mail, so I decided to write a little more later and send it by the air mail that would bring it back home about the same time as it would have arrived if it had been posted in the usual way. I did not get any more writing done, for on Sunday I got my temperature taken and had to give up the English service. Since then I have been unwell and ill with a temperature that has ranged from about 96° to about 105°. I think the bout is now over and I'll be allowed up tomorrow. At any rate, long before this reaches you I should be at the "talking" again.

I hope you have got settled down to the new term and that you like the books and the teachers. It is a pity that Mittens did not return to the home of his childhood and of so many happy years. We need never believe "The Cat Came Back" again. I hope Rab has not done any more wandering.

The weather is now cold here. Mr McNeill told us that there was hoar frost on the ground early this morning. Yesterday was the date of our wedding and I told Mother that if I had felt the same twenty-one years ago on the 7th of January, we would not have been married! ------ that day.

Give my love to Emily, Selina, Margaret and Eleanor, Evelyn and Joan. I think they are all the girls I know.

Dearest love to yourself, Daddy

22

Anand,
January 15th 1937

Dear Jack, Honor, Robin and Billy,

I hope the airmail reached you as soon as an ordinary letter would have done if posted in time. I was in poor form that week and the airmail I hope retrieved the situation. I hope that you are all well and settled down after the holidays. Jack was much in our thoughts on Sunday and Monday. I hope he has got over the high jump without knocking down any bricks.

There was not much to do at Lunawada. The first evening we went for a walk round the lake, nearly empty alas. On one of the banks there is a sacred tomb of some Mohammadian saint. He is believed to have power over evil spirits, to cast them out. People with various sorts of mental disorder come there at certain times and do a sort of penance. We saw several poor afflicted women seeking help. Some of them were sitting on the ground, shaking their head forward and backwards with some violence. It is a special thing called "dhua" and is regarded as a method of getting the mastery over evil spirits. Sometimes the person swoons and often there is an improvement afterwards. While they were shaking their heads a man was beating a drum. Another woman was walking backwards and forwards with a great swinging movement in front of one of the doors. She was as restless as a hyena in a cage. An onlooker told me that she was quite well at times and that the spirit began to persecute her. He believed that in the long run, when it was his pleasure, the saint in bliss would release her. We had a long talk about it but we did not get anywhere. These people say God is so great that he has no time for little things, so he entrusts some things to his courtiers and if you want to get near him you must approach him through them. I said that Jesus told us to go straight to God and say "Our Father", but my words were wasted. It was a relief to leave the place and go on to the other side of the pond. There we saw a lovely sight, the big golden full moon rising behind the trees coming up and making a street of gold on the water. As it rose higher the street or stream of gold gave place to the clear reflection of both moon and stars.

My duties at Lunawada were to give an address to the Christians, mostly Mission workers, their wives and families and baptise a baby. There was a prize distribution to the few children of the school, a visit to the homes of two teachers, where we made a pretence of drinking tea.

Coming out of one of the houses in the darkness of night I saw a lovely picture through the doorway of a mosque. It was the sky and full moon framed by the doorway, with a graceful palm tree at one side of the picture...

I retired to knit up the ravelled sleeve and prepare for an evening service in English at the railway institute. The subject was "Seek first the Kingdom of God" but my brain was like an engine that refuses to start no matter how much of the battery you use on the self-starter. The day seemed awfully cold, and all the works were frozen. I made so little progress that I decided either to cry off or else go and depend on God to fill my mouth with something at the time. The day seemed so cold and I was so miserable that I slipped out to Mr McNeill and asked him to take my temperature. He did so and there it was. Not very high but enough for him to say, 'You go to bed and I'll take the service.' I nearly jumped for joy and it did not take me long to go to bed.

Writing to Billy I said that a monster that had dogged my steps at Kathiawar pounced upon me at Dohad. So he did and with one cruel paw on my head and another on my stomach he held me faster than Livingstone's lion and a lifetime longer! He made my brain reel and stagger. It went out of my body altogether, and got tied to the fastest aeroplane that ever flew through space. Day and night it whirled me up and down, hither and thither, over and across as Icarus must have been whirled in the fiery chariot of the sun. Meanwhile my brain was tortured by the monsters, the liver was tortured by pecking crows, of the man whom Virgil saw damned in Avernus (consult Jack!). While this rampage was going on the beastly monster with his other paw turned my stomach upside down and inside out not once but several times. He was a devilish monster. On Tuesday morning he made pretence of leaving me, and with beaming smiles my would-be rescuer Dr Hazlitt declared that I was free. On the strength of that Mother and Miss Rogers were conveyed to Jahlod to fulfill the arrangements there. All through Mother was a brick and as bright and cheerful and helpful as she could be. In the afternoon Dr Hazlitt came in to see me. He found that, as I well knew, the beast after crouching in the morning had made another desperate spring and had sent my temperature spinning to 105° That caused a flutter and the doctor decided that a grand and gallant effort must be made to shoot the cruel raging savage beast. He concluded that at least fifteen shots fired three times a day, for five days would be needed. So the shooting began with strong yellow tablets that looked really dangerous…

Two days later RHB was able to get out of bed and go for a slow walk…

"… for which I had neither permission nor prohibition." When Mr McNeill and Dr Hazlitt heard of this they all came in as solemn as "waits" at an old-time funeral. Hugo looked solemn and swallowed something that looked like gruel or anger or anxiety. Mave held her chin up and I could see the point of her nose visibly rising. JH looked dour and his long moustache dropped an inch and looked ten times more grizzly than usual. I maintained an even calm and when they were at their glowering gloomiest I said:

'Hugo, I read a lovely story yesterday showing the limitation of knowledge. A little girl learned all the tables up to 12 times 12 = 144. Her grandfather could not catch her out even in seven times. Then he said to her: How much is 13 times 13? She looked at him scornfully and said "Grandfather please do stop your nonsense. There is no such thing".

The frigid scowls were melted, a cracking smile broke through and Mave only said, 'That's a nice way of getting out of it.' I replied, 'Look here. I have often walked ten miles and preached twice with that same temperature and it never did me any harm.' Still I resolved not to cause them any more alarms and I led a quiet peaceful life, harmless alike to others and self until the time came for me to leave Borsad. Grateful I am for all the attention I received there. I obediently supped hot water and bicarbonate of soda, drank sweet milk diluted with soda water, Horlicks malted milk, glucose and all the queer things like that. Soon I got chicken soup and a piece of the chicken that had walked through it in the pot, and best of all scrambled eggs once a day.

We had worship on the verandah before we separated, and I found that when I began to read my voice was as low as a crow with a cold in its throat. Mr McNeill's car was out of action so Miss Breeze drove up to Dohad station. We got a carriage all to ourselves and another of the same from Gidha to Anand, which we reached at eight o'clock. Dr Hanna met us and we spent a very happy restful night there. I stayed in bed till two o'clock. Dr Hanna inspected me and told me, 'Take it aisy' at Cambay. That I am doing, having the time of my life resting much and feeding often. Before the week is up I'll be as fat as a turkey, and as full of life as a deer on the plains, or a game-cock or an Arab charger. The goodness of Mother and the kindness of John and Lily is beyond thought or expression. Here ends the epistle, which, keep with the others. Uncle Willie might like to see it.

Love to you all from Dad

Anand, Surat and Broach

23

Anand
25th January 1937

Dear Honor, Robin, Billy and Jack

We had a great week of rest in Cambay. Except for a short walk in the fields and a jaunt to look at the Mahi River, I never stirred out of the bungalow. Before the end of the week I was feeling quite strong again and got up in the morning and stayed up all day. The presbytery was to meet in Anand on Wednesday the 26th. We had just time to get there by the afternoon train. A number of people were at the station including Jack's correspondent. When we arrived in Anand we beheld a gay scene. The compound was decorated. There were several arches. The first one had a large WELCOME in English. Another one had a Gujarati inscription, gold letters on red cloth. The designer and executer has given it to us as a memento. The bamboo sticks holding up the arches were decorated with big leaves of the banana tree. The church was crowded. An address was read and a little silver box presented. We were garlanded and bouqueted, and I had to give an address. It was a very pleasant enthusiastic meeting and we met many old friends whose hands we touched.

> *The presbytery meeting was a formal affair, during which RHB talked of celebrating the centenary of the Irish mission in 1941 and proposed a visit by representatives of the Indian Christians to Ireland (In his books RHB tells of how the war postponed this visit, but it eventually took place in 1947 when RHB was Moderator). After many meetings RHB and AHB went to Montgomerypur at the invitation of a close friend, Rev Samuelbhai.*

The church was built after the floods had washed away the old one. It is well built, a little too good perhaps, considering the position of the people. I would rather have a smaller, plainer one built by the people themselves than these grander ones built by foreign friends.

When we were about to come away we were invited in for tea. There were delicious *puris* and other Indian cakes, lots of apples, oranges and bananas, and very good tea. When it was beginning to get dark we started home. Mr Beatty drove till he came to a railway crossing. The gates were closed and locked from the station. 'When will the train come?' 'In ten or fifteen minutes.' That would take us halfway home. We backed and turned and went down a lane to the right, were told that it led nowhere, backed again, got the car astride a hump on the road, got over it with a scraping sound on the exhaust pipe and other underworks. We got near Anand and were driving along by the side of the pond. Finlay Stewart, who was with us, and I, simultaneously gave the alarm, 'Watch! Another hump!' It was too late. The driver did not see it. We were on it. The front wheels went over on one side. The bottom of the car scraped along the top and stopped, suspended.

We all got out, called a dozen men. All together with a great effort and a mighty noise lifted the front wheels up and pushed the car back. It was a hard job. I had looked at the brake to see that it was not on. It was not, but still the car was mighty hard to shove. When it did move back we learned the reason, for as soon as it got a strong push off the mound and backward down the slope, the engine started and the car almost bolted. It was in reverse gear, and it was no wonder so many men were required to move it. We thanked the men, said, 'Many hands make light work' etc. and went on our way again. We reached the mission house safely. I have often wondered why Mr Beatty has so many adventures and hair breadth escapes to tell about. I know now!

One morning Mother and I went out for a walk in the fields behind the bungalow. We often walked there in bygone days. We walked in the deep dust of the back road till we came to a gap in the hedge, aY made by a forked stick like the merrythought (or bone) of a chicken. We went through it and as we were making our way to the shade of a row of mango trees, a woman overtook us. We spoke to her and she asked us to come along to her garden. We followed her along a field and through one of two gaps. The path led along by the side of a plot of sugarcane, ten or twelve feet high and growing so thick and close that a man or a cow or a horse could be hid in it a few feet away from the edge.

We went on till we came to the house, built in the fields, or made mostly from branches and thatched with palm leaves. Two buffaloes and a calf were tied outside in a byre. We were told that they were churning in the house. We were invited to go in and see it. They explained everything to us and were most friendly. The churn was a big black clay vessel. The staff had a rope twisted round it so that it turned round inside the churn when the two women pulled the rope turn about. Now and again the lid was taken off and water poured in it. While doing that one of the women put a hand – not too clean – into the churn and lifted up a handful of the milk to see if the butter had come!

There were two boys in the house, cousins, both of whom go to school and study English, one in the fourth and the other in the third standard. I asked them to show me their reading books and read for me. One of them read a bit of John Gilpin and the other read something about Scōtland. I tried to get him to say Scŏtland but I didn't succeed. When we were coming away the man of the house and the boys loaded us with sugar cane and two papayas. They would have given us as much as we could carry if we allowed them. And all because we came from Dr Hanna's hospital.

Tuesday was the day of our departure. Breakfast was at 8.30 so we were up and had our suitcases, holdall, baskets, handbags, etc. all packed and ready before that. One of the men took our baggage to the station and had our tickets ready for us when we arrived in Dr Hanna's car. We got the Kathiawar Express, one of the best trains on the line, and leaving Anand at 9.21 we were at Broach at 11.49. There was an Indian gentleman in the carriage, but I was tired with all the talk of the week and I only bade him "the time of day". I had type-written copy of the old minutes of the presbytery (1843–75) with me and I read it all the way, only looking out once or twice to look at the course of the Mahi River towards Dewan, and at the huge piles of snow-white cotton at Palij station near Broach.

It was delightful to be with the Lyles, and to see the great river Norbudda, with the railway bridge, a mile across, way in the left, the palm groves on the other side, and the triangular sails of the boats coming or going towards the sea. Our bedroom door opens out into the compound with the river in the front. Early in the morning we see the most glorious sunrise, and in the evening the sunset surpasses words. The weather is warmer, 94° in the shade in Ahmedabad, but there is a pleasant breeze from the river and an open view that makes one long for a house in the country, facing south, with a room looking east and another west! There let me stop!

Love to all,
Dads

24

Broach
29/ 1/1937

Dear Honor,

We are having a delightful time with the Lyles. They got their home mail today. We will not get ours till we reach Surat tomorrow evening. It is hard to realise that your last letter has gone to us in India! It will be great to meet again after six months of separation. From here we go to Surat, Borsad, Ahmedabad, Bhavnagar. In Borsad I have to take the service on "Hospital Sunday". We are both very well and hope you are well also. It will not be long till we see you. I hope the storms will be over before we sail.

Love to Emily, Selina, Jordanstown and all the rest. None the less for "Eyebright".

Your loving Dad

P.S. If you have any BLUE stamps keep one for me. I haven't received one. They are scarce.

"Fooled" Again

25

Surat
Feb 2nd 1937

Dear Boyd family,

The clock has moved so swiftly and the days have sped as fast that it is Tuesday the 2nd of February before I got pen to paper to write to you. Where did the days go? Well on Friday we had the reception in Broach Church. The church bell was rung and a large congregation filled the church. The pastor presided. Nurses sang the song of welcome. We were garlanded and the address, printed on beautiful white satin, was read and presented along with some other gifts. I thanked them and gave a full arm's length address on various subjects.

We had to leave Broach at 9.49 on Saturday morning and packing had to be done. We went to bed early in order to be up and get all done in time. We were ready on the minute, went to the station, were garlanded again by those who came to see us off. We took our tickets for Kim station at which we got out. I had been there before – the first time with Dr Scott, in 1910, when we cycled from Kim to Arett, a distance of eighteen miles on a bad road. He told me awful tales of the Great Famine and how the children were forsaken by their parents and left by the wayside to die till he and Dr Shillidy came and rescued them. I got to know some of the children whose lives were saved at that time and I have met some of them again.

In the following year I went more than once from Kim to Surat and on to Arett on a bicycle. Once, when returning, there came a sudden unexpected shower, like a waterspout, that drenched me to the skin. I had no change of clothes with me and so I got into the first train that came – a goods – and got a seat with the guard in the van. I hung out the clothes to dry and before I reached Surat I was as dry as when I had left Arett. Once I sent the cook out at four in the morning in order that he might have the house and dinner ready for me on my arrival in the evening. He got to Kim by the morning train, but from there he could not get a cart, as the arrangements that had been made for one had broken down, so that when I reached Kim in the evening I found him there concluding a bargain with a man who had agreed to take him to Arett. The dinner was late that evening and I had to wait for a long time before my bedding arrived.

How different things were this time! Mr and Mrs Lyle were with us, and the lady missionaries of Surat had kindly sent out their car twenty-five miles – to serve us for the day. We all left our baggage with the station-master, got into the car and were driven six or seven miles along good road. Then we branched off into a cart track through the fields, towards Varethi. We had not gone far along it when we were stopped by a small group of people, not dacoits, far from it; indeed, they were good friends – the Hindu doctor of Tadkeshar, his wife and family and Manjibhai, the compounder of the government dispensary and his family. He was one of those orphans. For many years he has been one of the most highly respected men in the community and a tower of strength to the Christians of the neighbourhood. I knew him in Surat a long time ago and it was a great delight to see him again. They garlanded all of us and invited us to their village for tea, but we had not time for that pleasure, so after a chat we went on our way refreshed by their great kindness.

We went on to a village called Morvan where some of the Bhils who became Christians a few years ago live. There we were hospitably received by the Patel of the village, a Hindu, who has been very friendly and has given a house for the Evangelist to live in and also a small plot of ground. We got out and went up three or four steps to the raised verandah of his house. There was a table on the verandah, and also several chairs. We were invited to sit. We had garlands again from our Hindu host and tea which was hot and refreshing. He showed us all over his house, which was very dark and cool inside, and brought us to the back room in which there is a little altar where he offers sacrifice to his chosen god whom he called "*agni Narayan*". The Latin scholar of the family will know that *agni* comes from a Sanskrit root and passes through Latin in the form of *ignis* and into English as ignite, ignition, etc. and means fire. Our friend told us that fire is the first quality of God and therefore he worships *agni Narayan* or the Lord Fire. I had a long conversation with him on the difference between a Person and a Thing. I told him that things have certain qualities like weight, shape, etc. and that fire has the qualities of light and heat. You cannot, however, say that fire is just, or kind, or forgiving; these are personal qualities. To us God is a Person and we can speak of His purity, His righteousness, His love, etc. and therefore we can have fellowship with him in a way we cannot have fellowship with fire. We can say that fire signifies or is a symbol of purity, enthusiasm, etc. but we cannot regard it in itself as a quality of a person or of God. It is a symbol, and in worship we get above the quality which it signifies. Of course, Billy understands all that conversation and Honor is green with jealousy because she was not there to hear it! Robin may wonder how many Sanskrit roots there were in it and how many of them have gone to swell the Latin vocabulary! I enjoyed the talk, really! and I think my kind friend saw what I was trying to get at.

We saw from his verandah some fine farm oxen, one of which had peculiar horns. Instead of turning up and out, they turned down and in and formed a circle or sphere round the animal's head, meeting behind the lower jaw. I never could draw anything but money out of a bank! So I can't give you a picture. I asked had they any special name and was told that they are called *mindu* (sing.) and *minda* (plural). The word means a dot, or a circle, or a ring round anything.

We got into the car again and drove on towards Varethi where most of the Christians live. We looked at the houses of the new Christians and spoke to as many of them as we saw. Then we went to the school where the preachers and teachers were waiting for us. There were nearly sixty girls and boys present, a number of girls being in the fourth class. Of course they knew we were coming and had on their best clothes and cleanest faces. They sang a song of welcome and of course garlanded us.

We had got so many garlands that we were getting accustomed to them, and might have been disappointed if they had not been given to us. The name of these garlands is *Phul* (Fool) *har*. The first word means a flower and the second a garland or necklace. My frivolous mind invented the wicked pun "Fooled again" when the garlands were put round my neck, but there was so much kindness in the intention of the givers that such a thought was a true sign of depravity such as the Westminster divines never fathomed. I had to say, 'Thank you.' How often have I said, 'our hearts are overflowing with joy,' and, '*tamaro abhar manijechhiye*'? One is not expected just to say that and sit down. Dear me, no. They would be cheated and wronged if his honour or hers did not make at least two remarks, so I supplemented the "thank yous" with a few sentences of our delight at seeing (i) their cleanliness (ii) the development of their minds (iii) the new Life that had come to them through Jesus Christ. I expressed the hope that some of the boys and girls would go on and study till they become teachers.

The sight of these children was the most precious thing I have seen in India next to the Christians at Sangela. I think they were even more impressive. Three years or so ago these people knew nothing about the Gospel and here are their children, some of them in the fourth standard, able to read and sing and answer questions about Jesus and the Gospel, living in a new and better world and some of them ready if they get the chance to become nurses or teachers or Biblewomen. I have heard a lot about village uplift, but that was one of the best examples of it I have seen. Jesus is the real uplifter, when those who say that they love Him go and obey Him by helping others.

From the school we went to the house of one of the leaders – a big house. It was ready for us. A rug was on the floor, a table was covered with a cloth and also two central chairs behind the table for us. Everybody came. The house was packed to the door and many sat outside. Hindu and Mohammedan onlookers were outside and one influential Mohammedan in the house. At first these people were persecutors, beat the Christians, fired shots at them, etc. Now they are friendly.

We had an address of welcome, more garlands and an address from the visitors. It was now getting late and we had an engagement to keep at the tent where food was being sent. A Mohammedan gentleman invited us to his house to drink tea. It was out of the question. I, for one could hardly stand, I was so tired, but he let it slip that he would be satisfied if we just stopped at his door. We agreed and when we did we found that he had ready a basket filled with garlands and bouquets and so we were "fooled again"! How different a man he is now from what he was when he stirred up the village against the Christians.

We now returned to the mango trees where the small tent was pitched. I sought its shelter and lay down on the carpet with a coat under my head and stretched myself for a few minutes. Perhaps I slept! I do not remember. At any rate it must have been a short sleep for I soon heard the welcome sound of dishes outside. We greatly enjoyed the meal and had time after it to potter and talk to the kind folk who had prepared it and brought it to our camp. We reached Kim station in good time for the two trains, one going north to Broach and the other south to Surat.

At Surat there were lots of people to meet us at the platform and of course there were garlands. Outside the high school, Boy Scouts were waiting with the band to receive us, and as soon as we approached them they struck up "God save the King"! A few words to the Scoutmaster and we were off through the streets of the city and soon reached the narrow lane, down which I often dragged weary feet, to the mission house.

The old entrance to the Press, the courtyard with fountain and goldfish and evergreens the same as ever – maybe the goldfish are new! A Press man told me that they are very old. The house I lived in is occupied by Miss O Neill and Miss Fullerton, the one Dr Scott lived in while I was in Surat and in which we had our wedding breakfast is closed at present. The one we are in is the new one built by Dr Scott in his closing years, and now occupied by the superintendent of the mission Press. It has lovely view of the Tupti River, from which it is separated by a strong wall and a little garden. There is a sort of promenade along the wall over which you can look. In the evening when the tide is in and there is a breeze, it is very fine, and the sunsets on the river are indescribably beautiful. There is a large island of sand, but it is almost covered at high tide. Nets are spread to catch the fish as the tide comes up and one can see the fishermen in their boats with lateen sails going up to glean the harvest of the river – and we can hear the temple bells ringing and the drums being beaten morning and evening. It is just Surat.

    Love to you all,
    Dads

Homeward Bound

26

Borsad
5/2/37

Dear Honor,

It is Friday Feb 5th. Next Friday will be the 12th, and the next the 19th. Letters written for that date will go by our boat, and will reach England as soon as we do. So where is the good in writing them? Better send an air mail. So there is only one more regular letter to write. I'll need it to bring the travelogue, of which you must all be weary, up to date.

We came here yesterday evening and had a rousing welcome from the band. We saw some things this morning, but have not been to the hospital yet. There will be a hospital service on Sunday which I am to conduct. I hope there will be a good collection!

PROGRAMME

Feb 8th–11th Ahmedabad
12–13th Bhavnagar
14–16th Abu
17th Mission Council; Ahmedabad
17th evening – to Bombay
20th Sail – Hurrah!

Love from Dads

27

Borsad 7/2/37

Dear Jack, Honor, Robin, Billy,

Here we are in Borsad about to go to Ahmedabad, our last station but one, and here I am starting to write the last regular letter that will sail from India before we do. It is hard to take it in, that the months have come and gone and that soon we will be counting the days of the last one.

We had a busy time in Surat, and as usual Sunday was a full day. The first engagement was the morning's service at about nine o'clock. The church was packed. It is a nice old church built by the London society missionaries and finished in April 1840, before our missionaries were appointed. It was well built, and will look nearly as well at the beginning of the second century as it did at the first. But there will be this difference that then it was empty and now it is overflowing. We were met at the door by the minister and two elders who conducted us to two chairs facing the congregation. Sitting in the Surat church reminded us of our wedding there in January 1915. The usual service had to be conducted and I was responsible for the sermon.

Later, RHB visited Sunday schools for Non-Christian boys and lamented the absence of teachers. The next day he was present at the opening of a new badminton court in the church compound.

It is being run by the young people's society and I had the honour of sending the first "feather across". Mother played in the first game, four on each side. The games went on for some time and the tables were put on the court and soon there was tea and various sorts of Indian sweets and cakes.

On Tuesday they visited the high school, where there were more speeches and games. In 1935 Britain had granted India a measure of self-government and some of school's old boys were now holding posts of responsibility.

When we arrived we were greeted with "The King" on the band and marched under a bridge made by scouts to the front. Mother distributed the prizes. A long and varied programme of songs, recitations, and scenes, including one from the *The Merchant of Venice*, was gone through. A Parsee play near the end was very funny. I could not make out all the words, but the audience laughed a lot. Shylock was good. There was a dinner attended by "all of us" and forty or fifty old boys and their wives. Some were Hindus, some Moslems and some Parsis. I never was at anything of the kind before. Some of the old boys spoke – a Parsee judge retired and recently appointed to be prime minister of a native state, also a Hindu wearing a white cap who is a Congress candidate for the Bombay legislative council. The following day was the girls high school. Mother distributed the prizes and made the speech – a most excellent one. On Thursday the first order of the day was to visit the English cemetery where the well-known tombs of the managers of the East India Company and also of British affairs in India are, for Surat, as no doubt you have read, is the cradle of the British Empire in India! The tombs are well-preserved and some of the quaint inscription tablets have been renewed. You can still read of the excellent lady who through the spotted veil of the small-pox rendered an unspotted soul to God. They were grand fellows in those days and enjoyed the pomp and splendour of their office. We also looked at William Dixon's memorial and some other graves that had a deeper personal interest for us than the tombs of the governors of the Surat Factory.

> *The next day they took the Kathiawar Express at 2.17 for Anand.*

It was that train on which we left Surat for Abu on our wedding day. We soon reached Borsad. When we got to the gate of the Christian quarter, "The Beautiful Garden", we saw the bunting and the arch and the people drawn up in two lines, and soon we heard the strains of the Borsad band. We heard nothing else! It was a traditional welcome. We had to get out of the car, submit our necks to the flower bearers and shake hands with many people, some of whom we knew – among them Hueba, whom you all remember!

She shed copious tears as she enquired for your health. In the midst of noise, dust, good wishes, smiles and greetings we processed to the bungalow which memory seethed with many a thought for "gone, gone, were the old familiar faces". Still, it was pleasant to be back again and it was not difficult to think oneself back into the past.

RHB preached on the text, "It is more blessed to give than to receive".

There were more visits to outstations, more garlands so that the car was full of flowers and it was getting dark, so we hurried back to Borsad. The first time I did it was on a horse with a very short back and a short pace. I was tired and sore, not so this time. Sunday followed and on Sunday evening we went to Anand, got some things out of our trunks and came to Ahmedabad which we are now leaving. It is six on Wednesday evening. We leave in an hour and a half, will spend the whole night on the train and reach Bhavnahagr – our last station– at seven in the morning.

Love to you all,
Dads

28

Bhavnagar
11/2/1937

Dear Honor,

It is now ten to nine. We arrived at Bhavnagar station an hour and a half ago. We have had "*chota hazri*" and a bath and are free until breakfast time at about eleven. After that the programme will begin. We go to Wallacepur at four, and the home mail must be out, or ready, before we go.

We enjoyed Ahmedabad, slept in our own old room in the house where you were born. We saw you there. And in the church where you were baptised, and along the road where we wheeled you; although you would not recognise the place. Well it is only a little more than three weeks now. So good-bye for the present, and overflowing love from

Dads

29

The *Viceroy of India*
Feb 27th 1937

Dear Honor,

Here we are in the blue waters of the Mediterranean Sea, with a calm sea, cool breeze and glorious sunshine. Mother went to Cairo for the day yesterday and had a long day from 7.30 a.m. to 10.30 p.m. travelling, seeing the Pyramids etc. I saw them in 1928 with more leisure. We who remained on the ship had a lovely day in the Suez Canal. All the other ships tied up to let us through. The biggest one we passed was the Orient liner, *Ormonde*. We had booked on it from Port Said but changed our minds when we thought over it. Soon after, Mother and Miss Rogers went away at Suez. I prowled around looking for letters, which I got. Many thanks to you all. I enjoyed them. The proposals which you make for July will receive "sympathetic consideration"! I liked two of the photos, one very much. Sorry you were not yet satisfied with your hair! A week from tomorrow we will be in London, I hope. We are travelling so fast, and this ship stays such a short time in ports that we decided to go all the way by sea to London, hoping that the last part of the journey may not be any more unpleasant than the long train journey the other way, which I dislike.

Till we meet, fondest love from
Dads

PART FOUR

2010-2019

Bangladesh/Phule Phule

When I was appointed as the European Union ambassador to Bangladesh in 2010 I was mindful that this country was part of India in RHB's time, and that I would be following in his footsteps. I followed RHB's advice and started learning the Bangla language. "Bangla-desh" means the land of Bangla, and the language is central to the country's identity. Uncle Robin, ever the language scholar, told me that the word Bangla has given two words in English – bungalow and bangles.

The Bangla language has similar Sanskrit roots to Gujarati and the word for flower is "Phul" – just like "Phul" in Gujarati.

One of my first tasks was to visit EU-funded projects to provide food security to thousands of people in the poorest parts of the country in the south and south-west. These areas are greatly affected by cyclones and sea level rise because of climate change.

Each time Paola and I arrived in a new village we were welcomed with garlands. We were deeply touched by the warm kindness of the poorest people we had ever met. Like RHB and AHB we were soon laden with garlands, or as he put it in his "wicked pun," "fooled again and again".

I soon became intrigued by the work of Rabindranath Tagore, the finest poet in Bangla. I found both an Irish and a Scottish connection. The Irish connection is W.B. Yeats, who was one of the first to discover Tagore's work. The Scottish connection is Robert Burns. Tagore adapted the words and music of one of Burns' most beautiful songs to the Bangla language and topography. He transposed "Ye banks and braes" into "Flowers and flowers" in "Phule Phule", today one of the most popular folk songs in Bangladesh.

On the day appointed for my first meeting with the prime minister of Bangladesh, Sheikh Hasina, I was sitting in a large room in her palace, dressed in my best pinstripe suit, talking nervously to her diplomatic adviser. I told him about Tagore and Burns and started humming the tune of "Phule Phule". At that precise moment the prime minister, wearing the most beautiful sari, appeared and sat down in a chair beside me. The adviser began the introductions by gleefully informing the PM that the new European Ambassador had a song for her. This was not the time to be shy. So I started singing "Phule Phule, dhole dhole". And then, for an unforgettable few moments, the prime minister joined in and sang the song, in a soft and fine voice. Perhaps this was how it felt for RHB when Mahatma Gandhi joined him in the singing of hymns.

Burma: The Path of Valour

Early the next year, in 2011, I travelled the short journey east to neighbouring Myanmar (Burma). I had long wanted to visit Burma to see where RHB's eldest son, my Uncle Jack, died in the Second World War.

One of my earliest memories is of Gran reading us the chapter from RHB's book *The Path of Valour*, which tells of Jack's death. I later read for myself the earlier chapters, the stories about John as a boy, walking with his father and with his dog, Rab, in Cushendun and Ballycastle, favourite family holiday places in County Antrim.

As a boy I stood to attention, by my mother's side, in the front pew at Windsor Presbyterian Church each year on Remembrance Sunday. We faced the memorial tablet, with the name Capt. J.H. Boyd at the top. My father read from the pulpit, and then we observed two minutes' silence, finally broken by a bugler sounding the Last Post.

Tears rolled down my mother's face and there was nothing I could do to comfort her.

My mother always regretted that no one from the family had been able to visit the place in Burma where her brother is remembered. Burma remained a closed country for many years, but by 2011 it was just beginning to open up. So this trip was for my mother.

Here is the letter I sent the Boyd family afterwards:

Dear Boyd Family,

Paola and I have just returned from our visit to Myanmar (Burma).

On 4th January we went to the Taukkyan War Cemetery. It lies just outside Yangon (Rangoon), beyond the airport, on the road north towards Pyay (Prome). It looked as I'd expected from the pictures and from visiting Commonwealth war graves in many countries. All over the world, these are quiet, beautifully kept places.

At the entrance there is a stone plinth inscribed "Their names liveth evermore", and beyond, a simple white cross. In the centre there is a walled pathway around a circle, where are inscribed, on one side, the words:

> *Here are recorded the names of twenty-seven thousand soldiers of many races united in service to the British Crown who gave their lives in Burma and Assam but to whom the fortune of war denied the customary rites accorded to their comrades in death.*

On the other side are the words:

> *They died for all free men.*

It was here that we found the name Captain Boyd, J.H., one of three British officers, in the company of hundreds of Sikhs, many called Singh, of the Frontier Force Regiment.

We also found a more detailed entry in a book, which Paola photographed.

I was disappointed that there was no separate grave for Uncle Jack, but we found none from the year 1942. The graves were from 1944 and 1945, when the Allied Forces returned and reclaimed the land occupied by the Japanese.

Paola and I were struck by how Uncle Jack's name was in the midst of the Indian Army, and I was reminded of the photo of him wearing a turban, that Uncle Robin showed me when we met on last Remembrance Day in Edinburgh.

After we had walked around the cemetery, Paola and I found a stone bench where we sat down. I read from Mum's Daily Light for the day, 4th January, and for the day that Uncle Jack died, Palm Sunday 1942, including the words "I have fought the good fight, I have finished my course, I have kept the faith; henceforth there is laid up for me a crown of righteousness". I then recited from memory the verse from the poem by Binyon:

> *They shall grow not old, as we that are left grow old;*
> *Age shall not weary them, nor the years condemn.*
> *At the going down of the sun and in the morning,*
> *We will remember them.*

Paola read the beginning of the last chapter of *The Path of Valour*, entitled "That Means Me".

> *On that fateful day when Hitler attacked Poland, John was returning from a holiday in Donegal. Having learned the news, he said quietly and simply to his father, 'I suppose that means me.' Soon afterwards he set his name down as a volunteer, and after some weeks of irritating delay, his decision led him into the ranks as a rifleman.*
>
> *A year later, being commissioned, he again set his name down for service in India, the land of his birth, and in a few months he was in the Frontier Force Regiment, stationed on the North West Frontier. When Japan entered the war he went to Burma: Rangoon, Mandalay, and Moulmein, through jungles and swamps and across rivers, enduring hardship and loss with rare cheerfulness, till on Palm Sunday 1942, he crossed that frontier which all men must pass before they can reach the fuller and fairer life that is to be.*
>
> *He was commanding a company, which had been put into the attack on a Japanese position. "His company, thanks to John's determined leadership attained their objective," but while he led his men he was mortally wounded by a mortar bomb and he died like a gallant soldier.*

We went to a nearby market and bought some red chrysanthemums, and returned to the cemetery, where we laid them on a gravestone inscribed "A soldier of the Indian army, 1939–45, is honoured here".

In my letter to the Boyds I went on to refer to events unfolding in 2011:

"You may have seen on the news that in the same week William Hague visited Myanmar, soon after Hillary Clinton, and spoke to Aung San Suu Kyi. This was the first visit of a British foreign secretary since 1955. There are now promising signs that the country is at last opening up to freedom and democracy. I had detected a change in the attitude of the Myanmar ambassador, who six months ago was cagey about giving me a visa, but is now being very friendly. And the Bangladesh foreign secretary confirmed to me that Burmese attitudes are changing, which may help us in trying to find a solution for the Rohingya refugees.

As Grandfather Boyd wrote, Uncle Jack volunteered the day that Hitler invaded Poland. But Poland did not win its freedom after the war – that took another forty years.

Perhaps this year, seventy years after Uncle Jack's death, the freedom which he fought and gave his life for is at last coming to this beautiful country."

Looking back on that letter I see how wrong I was about the hope of change in the Burmese attitude to the Rohingya. A few years later the Burmese military was responsible for a genocide, sending these poor people, one of the most neglected groups in the world, to flee into neighbouring Bangladesh where they are not wanted.

The Path of Valour is RHB's finest book.

RHB's style is, as always, clear and straightforward. He transmits great love through simple storytelling. Jack appears with his father in several chapters. We see them together *one rainy day walking on the old road from*

Cushendun to Cushendall in a leisurely way, looking here and there for scraps of beauty that reward the loiterer who keeps an open eye.

And the story of throwing stones into a pond has stayed with me ever since Gran read it to us at Sans Souci Park on a Sunday afternoon long ago:

> One day a little boy and his father went for a walk. They lived in the city, but they loved the country, and went to see it as often as possible to see the green fields in which sheep and cattle and horses grazed; the hedges and the trees and the wildflowers; but best of all they liked to look at running water, to watch the ripples on its surface when a breeze stirred it, or the reflection of sky and tree and bird when it was calm as a mirror. Sometimes they saw a trout leaping, or were rewarded by the sight of a shy water hen stealing out of the reeds, or by the flashing splendour of a kingfisher.
> On this occasion they walked across fields till they came to a quiet pond. As they proceeded along the bank, the father saw a big stone. He lifted it, raised it high above his shoulder, and said to the boy: 'Now, watch, till you see the big splash I'll make.' He counted 'one, two, three, and away,' and flung the stone as far as he could into the pond. There was a big splash. Then he said to the boy: 'Watch the ripples. See how far the waves will go.' They gazed in silence while the circles became wider and wider, and then the boy cried out: 'Look! They have gone to the far side of the pond.'

> *They walked along again, with eyes open and ears intent. Then the boy picked up a small stone, and imitating his father, he said: 'Look, and see the splash I'll make.' He raised his hand high above his shoulder, counted 'one, two, three, go!' and flung the stone as far as he could into the pond. There was a splash and there were ripples. The boy watched the widening circles with growing excitement, and cried out, 'Look, daddy, look, my circles have gone as far as yours.' And that was true, for the eddies which the smaller stone made also went to the far side of the pond.*

My mother said that when the telegram arrived, bearing the news of Jack's death, it was the only time she saw RHB cry.

A few years later in 1947, when RHB was Moderator, the tablet in memory of those members of Windsor congregation who died in the Second World War was unveiled by Her Excellency the Countess Granville, the wife of the governor of Northern Ireland. RHB conducted the service and dedicated the memorial. In his address he said:

> *Time and again the world has gained control over individuals and groups of men, who, while others slept, have organised themselves into a system inspired by demonic energy and ruthlessness. Many of us have in a lifetime twice seen it almost succeed in bringing the whole human race under its proud and cruel dominion.*
>
> *It failed, and here today we recall with grateful hearts the unselfish heroism of a few out of many*

who halted its onward march with their young lives; and, in the presence of Almighty God, we honour their memory. Hatred was alien to them. War they abhorred. They saw the confused issues no more clearly than others, but they had a sense, a recognition of something beyond mere understanding, and they followed it till their goal was reached and their work was done.

This saved us from the cruel dominion of a view of life that has no more regard for personality than a stonemason has for the blocks that he hews and cuts till they fit his design. From that they preserved us, by toil and sweat and blood and dear life.

To what end? They secured for us a chance, an opportunity that we might show humanity how to live, not according to the selfish, sensual, materialistic principles of this world, but after the spirit of liberty, tolerance, kindness, brotherly love.

That message is as relevant today as the day it was written.

Gujarat

The following year, 2012, I was able to travel to Gujarat to see for myself where RHB had worked and lived and where my mother was born. I kept a diary of my visit.

Ahmedabad
3rd November 2012

My first impressions of Gujarat, arriving late at night, are in comparison with Dhaka, where I have been living for almost two years. Here there is a taxi service. There we only have rickshaws. Here the roads are in good repair and people travel on motorbikes. Whole families are on motorbikes. Women and girls too. You would never see that in Dhaka.

I am reminded of Kapuściński's first arrival in India, having to wait for the road to be cleared of people sleeping on the tarmac, the only place where they can lie down. Street life, nightlife, different shops.

As I was growing up in Windsor Manse we were surrounded by India. It was everywhere – in the brass table in the drawing room, in the elephant bell we used to summon the family from distant rooms to dinner, and in the tea chests in the box room, filled with pictures and carvings, and ivory elephants. My parents took my brother John and me to see our first film, at the neighbouring Majestic Cinema, a documentary about the Queen's visit to India. Uncle Robin and his family came home on furlough from India every five years, importing their exotic subcontinent into our grey provincial lives.

My mother was born in India – in Ahmedabad. At school, when I proclaimed this fact, my friends said that made me half Indian. When I was ten years old I used to wear a Parsee hat given to me by one of our Indian visitors. Mum and my sister Anne Louise visited India in 1965. They returned with yellow-boxed slide photographs, which we viewed projected on a wall. They had seen snakes and survived unheard of temperatures – 104° F in the shade. They were even interviewed by the BBC at Heathrow airport on their return.

Amartya Sen, in *The Argumentative Indian*, characterises foreigners' views of India and how they influence even Indian perceptions. In a chapter on Indian traditions and the Western imagination he describes "curiosity, power and curatorial approaches". My own curiosity was kindled at an early age.

I have brought *The Argumentative Indian* with me to Gujarat as suitable reading – while Paola chose *The Lonely Planet Guide*.

Over breakfast I feel confused, trying to read the books Uncle Robin has given me about the missionaries and the Irish Presbyterian Church they represented. I am nervous, just like before an important meeting, unable to take any more in, waiting for the event to begin.

Will it be a disappointment? Will there be nothing to see? Is this pilgrimage all a mistake? Then I feel a wave of emotion that I will be today seeing the house my mother was born in.

Why is this visit important to me?

Paola says, 'Because the line stops with you.' Does it? Does it not go on?

This visit is about finding RHB, but also about my mother, who died in March 2010. And it is also about finding me. My living and working today in Asia has something to do with my Indian connections.

But what about my religion? How do I reconcile my own beliefs today with those of my parents and grandparents, none more certain than RHB? How do I face those that do not share this faith? Today the main criticism of missionaries is that they tried to change the faith of Hindus and Muslims. How do I talk to Muslims in Bangladesh and let them know that my grandfather was a missionary? Should I apologise? Should I try to explain?

Maybe there are two answers. One comes from Hinduism itself – which I found in Sen yesterday: "It is not what you say you believe but what you do that is important".

And the other answer may come from my research during this visit – what remains today of the missionaries' work – the evangelism, the health care or the education?

Is there a lasting legacy, one to pass on to my children and grandchildren?

Later

We have changed hotels and I'm now having lunch on the verandah of the splendid MG, a beautiful old colonial house converted into a hotel, in the centre of Ahmedabad. There are heady perfumes from the stalls, horns honking outside, and delicious snacks with flavours I have never tasted before.

We arrived at the Irish Presbyterian compound on time, but we couldn't find the right entrance. As Uncle Robin advised, I asked for the bishop, and we met him in the main house. At first he seemed uneasy. He has only been bishop three months, and did not seem to understand why I was there. He chirped up when we discussed our plans for a week's trip round Gujarat, visiting the places RHB lived and worked in. We agreed with his suggestion to add a day staying in Anand and one in Borsad.

We walked over to the compound to see the house my mother was born in. Under a giant spreading mango tree was an old redbrick rambling bungalow, built in colonial style. Today there was a film crew working in it and we talked to the film star. The film was about organ donation, and it was being produced by an NGO. It wasn't a film against organ donation, as I first thought, but in favour of it. I was perplexed.

We entered the adjacent Bible centre. It was a more recent building, and modern Indian music was playing.

The librarian remembered Uncle Robin well and named many of the missionaries. He showed us an impressive collection of Bibles and translations going back to the early missionaries of 1840.

At the end of the visit the custodian of Bibles wanted to say a prayer and he asked to see my card, so that he could add a personal touch. When he saw my diplomatic title he decided to integrate political affairs into his conversation with God. It felt right that we were today talking direct to God. We often did that in my family. My father was a master of the spontaneous prayer.

We returned to the main building. I recognised it from pictures as Stevenson's College, where they trained ministers and where RHB was principal. As we walked towards the archives I noticed a beautifully carved stone window with symbols of the cross and the Irish harp. This touched me. I have seen images of this window often before. One panel is stencilled on the cover to *The Prevailing Word*. Someone in the Boyd family must still have a silver replica – gifted to RHB. We sat in the simple unadorned chapel. It was soberly Presbyterian. On the lectern were the signs of Alpha and Omega, as there still are in Windsor Presbyterian Church in Belfast. There was a pulpit, a communion table, and tall windows with high arches.

Our guides showed us round well-kept archives. This was Uncle Robin's recent work. I remember cousin Chris Boyd visited here in the 1990s and he told me that at that time the place was badly run down. Today it is well preserved and cared for.

Important people were born in Gujarat. Gandhi – the father of modern day India; Jinnah – the father of Pakistan;

and more recently Narendra Modi – the new Indian President. And on 2nd August 1921 my mother, Mary Honor Boyd, named after Honoria Lawrence, an intrepid observer of India in the 19th century, was born here too.

Rajkot
4 November 2012

We took the Saturday evening train from Ahmedabad to Rajkot, found a smart hotel and had a good meal. We slept in the next morning, and just had time for a rushed breakfast before an elder of the church picked us up and took us to Rajkot Church, for the morning service.

The church dates from 1880 and is solidly constructed – it survived the 2001 earthquake – but uninteresting. We took our shoes off at the entrance to the east transept and were introduced to the pastor, busy robing himself in the vestry. He wore a white cassock and red stole, which reminded me of the robes Uncle Robin used to wear when he was on furlough and preaching at Windsor. Somewhere along the way the Presbyterians in India discarded their black Genevan garb.

There were a couple of dozen people in the church and at first I thought that the congregation was going to be small. As they sang Indian songs I pondered whether the missionaries' work had been in vain, and thought too of the empty pews in many Presbyterian churches in Belfast today. At one time the *Belfast Telegraph* on a Saturday evening carried announcements of the next day's service from seventy churches – and that was just the Presbyterian congregations.

But, here in Rajkot, gradually the pews filled up with people of all ages, men and women, boys and girls. I later counted about 150 people.

The minister conducted the service in the Gujarat language. I could tell, by familiarity with the order of things, and by the tone of voice, when the congregation was saying the Lord's Prayer, and when they were reciting the Creed. The music was made by players of a tabla and a harmonium – such as also accompany Bengali music – and the congregation sang cheerfully. As well as Indian tunes, there were also choruses – including one I recognised from my Sunday School days.

At the end of the service the minister introduced us and asked me to speak. The minister interpreted for me:

My name is William Hanna and this is my wife Paola.

We live in Bangladesh, but I have come to Gujarat because many years ago my grandfather Robert Boyd came here as a missionary.

He lived in India from 1909 to 1922.

My mother was born here, and yesterday in Ahmedabad I saw the house where she was born.

We are going to spend a week visiting Gujarat seeing the places where my grandfather worked.

I am happy to see so many people in the congregation today.

I don't know Gujarati, but I have understood something about this service.

I understood "Jesu" and "Alleluia" and heard "Count your blessings" – and the Psalm tune "Duke Street".

> *If my grandfather Boyd were here today – and I believe he is with us here today – I am sure he would be pleased with this service.*

I think RHB would also have been pleased with me for being brief, although I don't know what he would have made of the quiver in my voice. I recall the address Uncle Robin gave at my mother's funeral. He delivered his well-chosen simple words slowly – he had become almost blind and it took him time to decipher the typed manuscript – showing great love and perfectly describing my mother's personality, but never flinching with emotion.

Back in Rajkot the service went on and on. It was remarkable to me how much was conducted by elders and how little by the minister. These were all articulate speakers, in no way shy, strong confident people proclaiming their faith. After two hours the service came to an end with communion – conducted in the Presbyterian tradition.

Afterwards the minister invited us to join him shaking hands with every member of the congregation. Each one greeted us with the phrase: "Praise the Lord".

We chatted with people who came up to speak to us – a senior government official, a dairy industrialist, and a young man who deals in visas. They took us to see the graveyard where Alexander Kirkland, one of the first missionaries, is buried, beside his infant daughter. The early missionaries were brave men and women.

Surat
7th November

During this trip to Gujarat one question has often been on my mind: a hundred years later, what remains of the missionaries' work?

A final paragraph in *Village Folk of India* talks of education.

> *Now come for a walk in the city. Let us climb up the rickety stairs of an old rambling house. See there are hundreds of Hindu and Mohammadian girls here. It is a school for high caste girls, and it is one of the finest sights to be seen in this city... Who are these bright intelligent young women teachers who are in sole charge of the school? They are Indian Christian women and girls, who have passed out of the Teachers Training College, and hold the highest Government certificate. What you see is one of Christ's greatest victories, the breaking of the bands of ignorance and superstition and the setting of the humble in places of influence.*

On Tuesday we arrived in Surat, port city and centre of the diamond industry. We stayed in a good hotel on the outskirts of the city and went to meet the contacts that Uncle Robin had given us.

In Surat the first Irish Presbyterian missionaries to India set up a compound in the heart of the old town. It was their centre before they established themselves in Ahmedabad. They built a church, a school, and a bungalow by the river. The church dates from 1840. It is simple and more beautiful than the one in Rajkot. The nave has tall broken-arched and louvred windows, permanently open to sunlight, breeze and noise. This was also the place where they placed the first printing press in Gujarat – built to print the Bible.

Uncle Robin lived in that bungalow in Surat in the 1950s, when Christian missionaries were still welcome in India. Some elderly people came up to talk to us. They remembered Robin, and Aunt Frances who played the piano, and my cousin Libby.

We visited the school on the same compound. It was today clearly separated from the church. The children were Muslim. This old area of Surat is predominantly Muslim, not Hindu. Visiting from Bangladesh, which is also predominantly Muslim, I felt strangely at home.

In Surat these days Christian children go to the Catholic school, which has a reputation for excellence. Muslims choose the Presbyterian school, because it is close by and there is no payment. We watched as an assembly of girls recited by rote "Every day I dance to the Lord", and "Yesterday, today and tomorrow I dance to the Lord." Did they understand a word of what they were saying?

We met the principal and toured the school. On the walls of the classrooms were pictures of Indian heroes, the poet Tagore, Nehru, the first prime minister of independent India, as well as Bose who led the fight against the British.

I knew that Surat was where RHB and AHB were married in 1915. I had brought a photo with me and spent a long time searching for the spot where it was taken. I had supposed that the steps in the picture were attached to a church, but today nowhere seemed to fit. In the end I decided that the place must have been in the corner of the old building which houses the girls' school.

I think this school must be the one that RHB describes in *Village Folk of India*. Today it has 2,000 pupils. However, while the church remains, today Indian law forbids conversion to another faith.

After lunch the friendly pastor told us of his family. He was from a jungle tribe and was proud that Uncle Robin had taught him English and theology. He remembered Robin as "a clever man who wrote the church history". He himself had been to Ireland and attended the General Assembly of the Presbyterian Church in Belfast. I was reminded that my friends from Windsor days, the Farises and the Rankins, one of whose ancestors, James Glasgow, was the first Irish missionary to India, still keep up the contacts between the church in India and Ireland.

The pastor had three children, one looking after mentally handicapped, one working with the blind, and one an evangelist. He was the first of his family "to come to Christ".

'Your grandfather planted a seed,' he said. 'And it grew.'

The next day we travelled to Anand and to Borsad.

In Anand we visited another Presbyterian church and saw the graves of past ministers and their young children. It was in Anand that RHB and Gandhi had shared that platform in 1915, urging young Indian men to answer the Empire's call. It was also here that Uncle Jack was born in 1917.

We saw around another primary school and then visited the St Stephen's Institute of Technology and Business Management. We were impressed. Here, alongside the old primary school rooms, was a new block, a tertiary level college, with 350 students and a young dynamic principal, Manish, who showed us the college's prospectus and its "mission statement". I was amused to discover a direct connection between "missionaries" and the "mission statement", a management tool I have often used.

In today's dynamic Gujarat of Narendra Modi there is great demand for the skills taught in the college. According to Manish, Stevenson College has the edge over others because of its emphasis on values.

'What values do you teach?' I asked Manish.

'Determination and focus,' the young principal replied. 'Young people today have no focus. Other colleges are just a business, but our college is about the students, we give them individual coaching. And the poorest get scholarships. We are less expensive and perform better than our competitors. That's why parents send us their children.'

In 1916 RHB wrote, "to help these lads get a good education under favourable circumstances and in a Christian atmosphere is one of the very best works the IP Church could do, and I hope there will never come a time when any stinginess on our part will prevent the poorer boys from receiving the education that is needed to equip them to play their part in the regeneration of India".

We toured the modern college, equipped with many computers, and we talked to a group of first-year students. They seemed keen and confident. After graduating they expected to move into good jobs. As we toured the college I remembered that it was the day of the US elections and asked who had won. 'Obama won,' they told me. I said to the students, 'Isn't that great news.'

'And we are honest,' added Manish. 'Because it knows we are honest, the state trusts the college to host exams even for students from other schools. They know we will not ask for payment.'

Later, at Borsad, where the hospital run by the missionaries was no longer in use, we met with a group of teachers and I asked them what was the legacy of the missionaries after so many years? They were unanimous in their answer. 'Education.'

Drumbo

On a hill in County Down, overlooking Belfast, stands Drumbo Presbyterian Church. Behind the church are the ivy-clad remains of a round tower, built by our forefathers to protect themselves from the raids of the Vikings. Next to the tower is a graveyard. Polished black or brown marble tombstones, with gold lettering, mark most of the graves. One tombstone is less shiny and stands out in its simplicity. The stone is rough granite, with black lettering. Here lie RHB and, by his side, AHB. Uncle Robin chose the inscription on the tomb from words of St Paul:

> *I determined not to know anything amongst you save Christ Jesus and him crucified.*

I stopped at Drumbo Church with Uncle Robin on a day in 2010 when we were on our way to visit my mother in a nursing home. As we stood by the graveside and looked northeast towards Belfast Lough, and Scotland beyond, he told me about RHB's last days. RHB had long suffered from angina, but in 1957 it got worse and my mother wrote to Robin in India that he should return to see his father. When Robin turned up at his parents' home in Osborne Park, Belfast, his father looked at him crossly and said:

'What are you doing here?'

'He was a single-minded man,' said Robin. 'He thought my place was in the mission field.' Robin went for a walk with his father down by the River Lagan, at Edenderry, soon before RHB died.

Robin returned to India and carried on RHB's work there in the 1950s and 1960s until it became difficult for missionaries to remain. He took the mission work further, to where it placed less emphasis on converting "the heathen" and more on seeking the good in all faiths, always with a special place for the Good News of the gospel. He worked tirelessly for church unity around the world, and was a noted ecumenist, directing the Irish School of Ecumenics in the 1980s.

In May 2018 when I paid my final visit to Uncle Robin in Edinburgh he was quite frail, and he told me of the night in October 1957 that his father died, peacefully in his sleep. Robin himself died a few weeks later.

*

We are coming to the end of this story about how, long after his departure from this life on earth, I came to know RHB, my grandfather, the missionary, writer and global traveller who started his journeys before cars and planes were invented.

Amartya Sen has described identity as "a quintessentially plural concept".

RHB had several identities. He was best known as the public figure, a writer who left enough traces on this earth to be studied by a researcher fifty years after his death.

But he was also the young child, sent away from home to live with relatives because his own family was too poor to raise him. He was the mischievous schoolboy whose teacher recognised that he had the brains to become a leader. He was the young man, so determined to become a missionary that he travelled to study in the USA, because he had heard that the queue would be shorter there. He was the brash young writer, telling of people in Manchuria he had never seen, and also the penman, powerful enough to persuade Annie Higginson to cross the world, during the First World War, to marry him.

RHB was an imperialist who called on young men to serve king emperor and country, but he was also his own man. He was proud of India's contribution to the war effort and was rewarded for his part in it. He never accepted the brutal face of Empire, but could only accept the sacrifice when his son, a captain in the Indian Army, was killed in Burma.

RHB was at heart a countryman, most at home in a village, or walking along a country road, in Ireland or India, and a writer whose best work is when he just tells stories. He fell in love with India. He learnt the Gujarati language and he learnt from his teachers about Indian philosophy. He met, admired and criticised the most famous Indian of all.

As his letters show, RHB was a father who dearly loved his children. They and his grandchildren and great-grandchildren have followed in his footsteps. Perhaps his great-great-grandchildren will also glean something from this story about him.

Justin Livingstone, the researcher into Robert Boyd's rhetoric discovered this final tribute, first published in the *Presbyterian Herald* in 1957.

> *Robert Boyd evoked love and respect. His friends knew him as one ever ready to help and encourage. His insight, common sense and decisiveness were a source of wisdom and strength to many. His integrity and conviction impressed themselves upon the whole church, which knew that these alone determined his voice and vote. A total stranger to all self-seeking, Dr Boyd never spoke for the sake of speaking, he seldom intervened in the debate in the General Assembly, but when he did, more often than not, it was to say the last word.*

Postscript

While Uncle Jack was soldiering in India, Uncle Robin also played his part in the Second World War. He joined the Home Guard – Dad's Army – and was posted to St Paul's Cathedral to look out for aeroplanes during the blitz. It was only when he was in his eighties that we learnt that he also worked as a code breaker linked to the Bletchley Park project. He had been headhunted by MI5 at his Belfast school, RBAI, because of his brilliance at mathematics and languages. I had often wondered why he was so fluent in German.

Uncle Billy was too young to take part in the war. Like his father he studied at Princeton University in the US and became a clergyman. He worked for peace and reconciliation in the heart of Belfast during the Troubles, and was awarded an honorary doctorate. Uncle Billy took up the Irish language in his retirement and, now in his nineties, is as enthusiastic, good-humoured and down to earth as his father was.

My mother spent the Second World War as a nurse in Belfast and in London. She broke her leg on the day of victory over Japan. Later she started training to become a missionary. However in 1947, when he was appointed Moderator of the General Assembly, RHB chose two young ministers to act as chaplains. One was Ray Davey, RHB's nephew, who had been a prisoner of war, and who later founded the Corrymeela Community. The other choice was less obvious. This was a rugby-playing friend of Ray's from Edinburgh University days, a young minister from the country congregation of Randalstown, called William Hanna.

What impressed RHB about Bill Hanna? Like RHB he was a farmer's son. He was an evangelical sort of minister, a great enthusiast and organiser, a prop forward who founded Randalstown rugby club, and sometimes appeared in the pulpit on Sunday with a black eye from Saturday's game. He also persuaded his country congregation to collect a record amount of money for the foreign mission. RHB wanted to reward this good example.

The story soon went round that there was something going on between Bill Hanna and RHB's daughter. When Bill Hanna was called as minister to Windsor Presbyterian Church, where RHB and his family worshipped, the rumours continued. It was not long before my mother decided that Bill Hanna should be encouraged to make a move. One day in 1951 he drove her to Glenann in County Antrim. Uncle Robin was the appointed chaperon. He recalled the day fifty years later, at my mother's eightieth birthday party:

In the car park at the top I had the wit to suggest that I should drive Bill's car down to the bottom of the glen and meet them there. And there I waited and waited. And so Honor became a minister's wife.

Bibliography

Anita Anand, *The Patient Assassin*, 2019.

Rev Robert Boyd, B.A., *Manchuria and Our Mission There*, Belfast, 1908.

Rev R.H. Boyd, *The Banyan Tree*, 1913.

Rev R.H. Boyd, *The Lonely Road*, James Clarke and Co, London, 1919.

Robert H. Boyd, *Village Folk of India*, United Council for Missionary Education, London, 1924.

R.H. Boyd, *Waymakers in Manchuria*, Church House, Belfast, 1940.

R.H. Boyd, *Couriers of the Dawn*, Church House, Belfast, 1940.

R.H. Boyd, *The Path of Valour*, Church House, Belfast, 1942.

R.H. Boyd, *Through Gates of Hope*, Church House, Belfast, 1947.

Robert Boyd, D.D., *Fuller Life*, Church House, Belfast, 1947.

Robert Boyd, D.D., *A Garland of Memories*, Church House, Belfast, 1949.

R. H. Boyd, *The Prevailing Word*, Church House, Belfast, 1953.

Robin Boyd, *Church History of Gujarat*, Dublin, 1980.

William Corkey, *Glad did I live*, Belfast, 1964.
Louis Fischer, *The Life of Mahatma Gandhi*, Jonathan Cape, 1951.
David Gilmour, *The British in India*, Allen Lane, 2018.
Arthur Hermann, *Gandhi and Churchill*, Arrow Books, 2009.
Ryszard Kapuscinski, *Mes Voyages avec Herodote*, Plon, 2006.
Justin Livingstone, Ambivalent Imperialism: The Missionary Rhetoric of Robert Boyd. *Literature & Theology*, Vol. 23, June 2009.
Julia Lovell, *Opium War*, Picador, 2011.
Pankaj Mishra, *From the ruins of Empire*, Penguin, 2012.
Madrushree Muerjee, *Churchill's Secret War*, Tranquebar, 2010.
Edward Said, *Orientalism*, Penguin, 1978.
Amartya Sen, *The Argumentative Indian*, Penguin, 2005.
Shashi Tharoor, *Inglorious Empire*, Hurst, 2017.
Shashi Tharoor, *Why I am a Hindu*, Hurst, 2018.
Muhammad Yunus, *Building Social Business*, Public Affairs, 2010.